IMAGES
of America

BOCA GRANDE

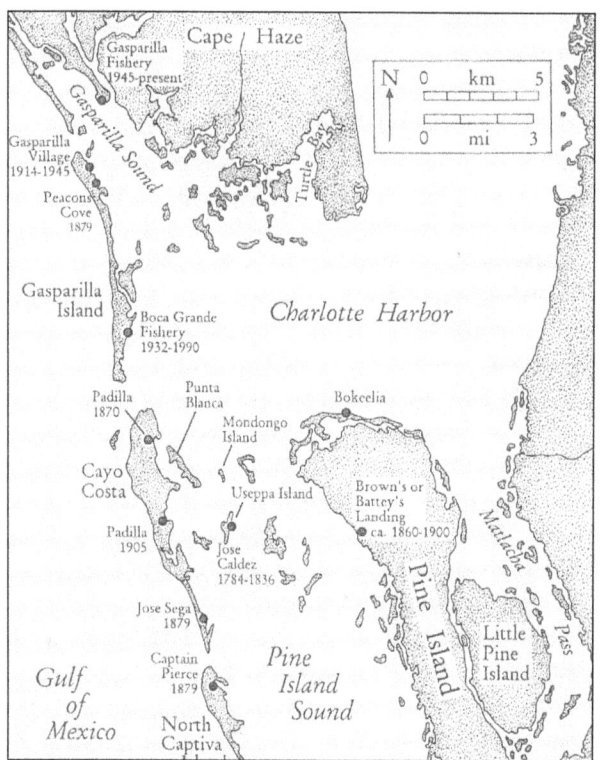

This map shows the sites of various fishing activities in the Charlotte Harbor archipelago in the 18th and 19th centuries. "Peacon's Cove" appears at Gasparilla Island's north end. (Map by Merald Clark, from *Fisherfolk of Charlotte Harbor, Florida* by R.F. Edic, reprinted with permission, IAPS Books.)

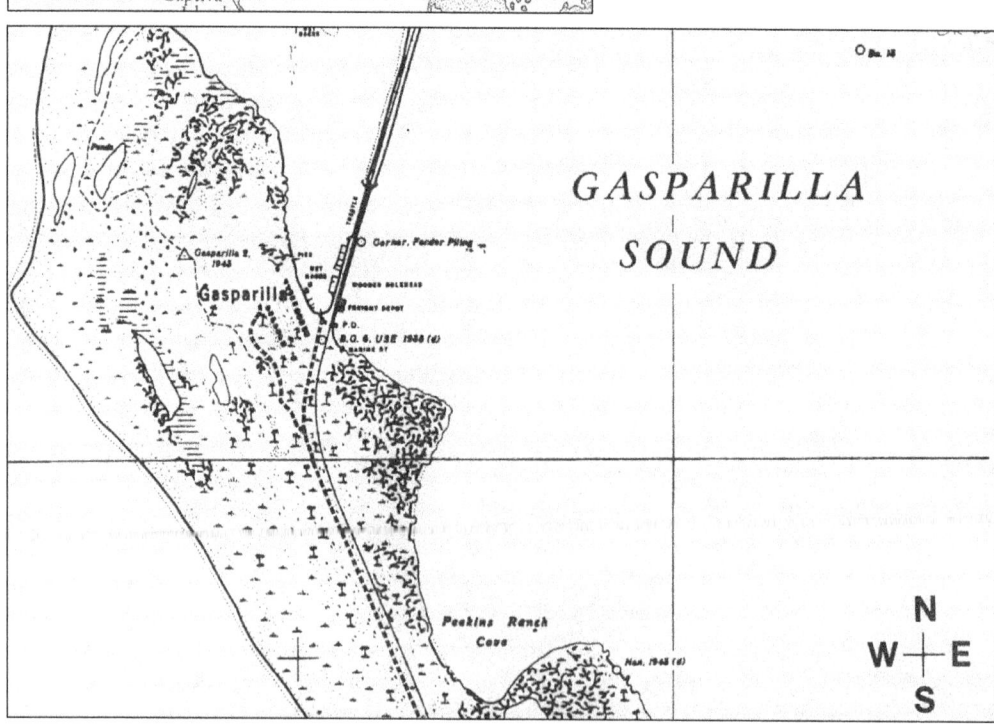

This enlargement of a 1939 map of the north end of Gasparilla Island shows the location of the now-vanished fishing village of Gasparilla. (From USCGS topographic map T-5859, published as an insert in C.D. Gibson's *Boca Grande: A Series of Historical Essays*, provided by Pat Nesser-Agles.)

Marilyn Hoeckel and Theodore B. VanItallie

Copyright © 2000 by Boca Grande Historical Society and Barrier Island Parks Society
ISBN 978-1-5316-0392-2

Published by Arcadia Publishing
Charleston, South Carolina

Library of Congress Catalog Card Number: 00-105335

For all general information contact Arcadia Publishing at:
Telephone 843-853-2070
Fax 843-853-0044
E-Mail sales@arcadiapublishing.com
For customer service and orders:
Toll-Free 1-888-313-2665

Visit us on the Internet at www.arcadiapublsihing.com

ACKNOWLEDGMENTS

This book is a joint endeavor of the Boca Grande Historical Society and the Barrier Island Parks Society. The authors thank the board members of both societies for their support and encouragement.

Individuals who generously made photographic images, maps, and other memorabilia available for the book include Homer Addison, Eunice Gault Albritton, Merald Clark, U.S. Cleveland, Pansy Polk Cost, Marge Dennis, Dr. Dennis B. Dorsey, Marguerite East, Robert F. Edic, Evelyn McKinney Ferguson, Peter Ffolliott, Charles Foster, Mark Futch, Jeff Gaines, Kay and Charles Dana Gibson, Charlyn Crandall Heidenreich, Dusty Hopkins, Michael Ingram, William H. Marquardt, Patti Middleton, Patricia Nesser-Agles, Suzanne Harris Savarese, and Joseph A. Savarese Jr. Photographic images and other memorabilia were also graciously provided by the *Boca Beacon*, the Boca Grande Fire Department, the Boca Grande Historical Society, the Boca Grande Lighthouse Museum, the Bradley Family Archives, the Charlotte Harbor Area Historical Society, Florida State Archives, the Gasparilla Inn, the Gasparilla Island Conservation and Improvement Association, Sarasota County Historical Resources, the Robert W. Johnson family, and the family of Charles Henry Williams.

We also thank Eunice Albritton, Doris Bishop, Pansy P. Cost, Marguerite East, Peter Ffolliott, Margaret Fugate, Stephen F. Seidensticker, Barbara Symon, and Sallie VanItallie for their helpful reviews of the manuscript.

Contents

Acknowledgments		4
Introduction		6
1.	Gasparilla Island's Fishing Heritage	7
2.	Two Lighthouses	17
3.	Phosphate, the Railroad, and Port Boca Grande	27
4.	Boca Grande: A Unique Island Town	51
5.	Getting There: Transportation on a Barrier Island	91
6.	Hurricanes	101
7.	The Beachfront	109
8.	Tarpon Fishing	115
Epilogue		127
Selected Bibliography		128

In one of the earliest known pictures of Gasparilla Village, c. World War I, men stand in front of the oil shed. In the background is Gasparilla's harbor with docked fishing boats and nets drying on racks. (Courtesy of the *Boca Beacon*.)

INTRODUCTION

By this book—with its antique pictures and memories of earlier years—we attempt to provide readers with a "time machine" that, when powered by the imagination, will help them recapture Boca Grande's remarkable past. We must start this process of "calling back yesterday" by remembering that, during the first half-century of its existence, Gasparilla Island was accessible only by water or via the Charlotte Harbor and Northern railroad trestle. In keeping with its island nature, it possessed a water taxi, a school boat, a library boat (the "book boat"), and a ferry service. Existence had a different rhythm in those days.

At the south end of the island, once a bustling port for the shipment of millions of tons of phosphate all over the world, there is now a serene state park. The venerable lighthouse, constructed in 1890, now contains a museum of local history. The railroad track, along which hundreds of freight cars bearing phosphate ore used to rumble, is now a bicycle and jogging path. The little fishing village of Gasparilla—the first habitation seen when the train crossing the long trestle over Gasparilla Sound finally reached land—has vanished. The old Boca Grande Hotel, which for many years stood so proudly on Gulf Avenue just to the south of First Street, is long since gone and has been replaced by Boca Bay's North Village. Happily, the Gasparilla Inn, Boca Grande's *grande dame*, still stands firmly upon the site where she began in 1911. Also, fortunately, the island's climate, its friendly inhabitants, its beautiful beaches, and its bounty of marine life (including the famed tarpon) still attract a small army of partisans.

When one takes the trouble to look for it, the captivating history of Gasparilla Island and its sole remaining town, Boca Grande, can be discerned just below the surface of today's exteriors. The old "Mercantile" still hides within today's post office. The waiting rooms and ticket counter are still "somewhere" within the confines of the remodeled railroad depot. Concealed inside the elegant community center is an unforgettable school, grades one through twelve. The experience of looking beneath these exteriors sets us off on a journey into the past that enriches the present.

One

Gasparilla Island's Fishing Heritage

The continuing history of Gasparilla Island is intimately tied to the rich bounty of the Charlotte Harbor estuary. The Calusa Indians were the first to exploit the marine environment, reaping enough fish and shellfish from the harbor to sustain a population of thousands. Then came the Spanish, and finally, in the latter half of the 19th century, fishing families from throughout Florida and the southeastern United States would migrate to the fishing grounds of Charlotte Harbor.

By the start of the 1700s, the shallow fishing grounds around Cuba and the nearby Caribbean islands were being depleted of their edible marine resources. These areas had been used to help feed the vast Spanish New World empire for 200 years. The Spanish Cubans needed a new source of food, and Charlotte Harbor was where they turned. The rich fishing grounds of the area were a source of high quality protein—mullet, redfish, pompano, grouper, trout, sea turtles—and these marine products could be cured and easily shipped to nearby Cuba. At first, the Cubans fished Charlotte Harbor seasonally, but it wasn't long before they began to settle in the area year-round. By the mid-1700s, semi-permanent fishing "ranchos" (fishing camps) were being set up and run in Charlotte Harbor by the Cubans. Local Indians were hired to harvest and cure fish for markets in Cuba. By the 1830s, various accounts report that up to 600 men, women, and children—Cuban and Indian—were working in about a dozen Cuban fishing ranchos in the harbor. The annual exports of four Charlotte Harbor fishing ranchos surveyed in 1831 were valued at $18,000.

In 1879, George B. Goode, an employee of the U.S. Commission of Fish and Fisheries, made a survey of fishing operations in Charlotte Harbor for the Smithsonian Institution. The Goode Report described four fishery stations on islands in the upper part of Charlotte Harbor: one on Captiva, one at the south end of "Lacosta" (Cayo Costa), one at the north end of Lacosta, and one at the northern end of Gasparilla Island.

During the year of the survey, the Gasparilla Island operation, headed by a "Captain Beacon" (Peacon) produced 550,000 pounds of salted mullet and 44,000 pounds of dried mullet roe. According to the Goode Report, Peacon's fish ranch had been active for at least two years prior to 1879 and was regarded by Goode as a "stable enterprise." Unlike the fisheries to the south, Peacon's fish ranch was described as having "buildings of a permanent character." The Peacon ranch was managed by Captain Peacon and his brothers and employed 30 fishermen, many of whom were known as "Conchs" because they came from Key West.

The fish ranch at the north end of Cayo Costa Island, just across Boca Grande Pass from Gasparilla Island, was founded and directed by Tariva "Captain Papy" Padilla and consisted of "23 Spaniards and one American," according to the Goode Report. Padilla, a native of the Canary Islands, had settled on Cayo Costa at the site of "Burroughs Ranch" (a small settlement that had been noted in an 1860 survey) in the early to mid-1870s with his wife, Juanita, and began catching and curing mullet for the Cuban market and probably for the Key West market as well. The Padilla operation, on what became known as "Tariva's Bayou," flourished until about 1901; Padilla family members continued to live and fish on Cayo Costa and on nearby Punta Blanca Island until the 1970s. Tariva Padilla is buried in a small cemetery on Cayo Costa. His descendants still fish local waters today.

In the late 19th century, the entire nature of commercial fishing in Charlotte Harbor was permanently transformed by the construction of an ice factory in Punta Gorda. In 1886, Col. Isaac Trabue (a founding father of Punta Gorda, just across the harbor from Boca Grande) had persuaded Florida Southern Railway, a component of the Plant System, to extend its line to Punta Gorda's dock area. Then, a few years later, a new ice-manufacturing plant was constructed by the Punta Gorda Ice and Power Company. It was soon producing 25 tons of ice per day and, at the same time, furnishing electric power to the town. (This company later evolved into Florida Power and Light.) The availability of an integrated railway system and insulated boxcars permitted the speedy transport of iced fish from Charlotte Harbor to cities throughout the eastern United States. During the ice plant's first full year of operation, 3.6 million pounds of fish were shipped out of Punta Gorda.

By the turn of the century, fish companies were operating at the "new" railroad wharf in Punta Gorda. The Punta Gorda Fish Company, the Chadwick Fish Company, and the West Coast Fish Company constructed fish buying and storage houses and ice stations throughout Charlotte Harbor. Many of these stations, as well as adjoining bunkhouses for the fishermen, were built on stilts over the water. These houses were designed to be serviced by "run boats" operated by the Punta Gorda fish dealers. The run boats carried a minimum of one hundred 300-pound cakes of ice.

Once the new system was in place for collecting iced fish from the ice stations, now widely scattered throughout the harbor, the traditional salt fisheries ceased to be viable. The Peacon Fish Ranch at Gasparilla Island's north end closed down in about 1916, and the Padilla enterprise on Cayo Costa changed from salting fish to simply catching fish for delivery to the ice stations. When the Peacon fish ranch closed down its salting and drying operations, some of the fishermen associated with the ranch moved to the shoreline of a small harbor just to the north of "Peekins Ranch Cove." This site became the thriving fishing village called Gasparilla. Before 1907, the village-to-be consisted of a cluster of camps and a few rickety dwellings for fisherfolk. However, with the completion of the Charlotte Harbor and Northern Railway (CH&N) line between Port Boca Grande and Arcadia in 1907, activity rapidly picked up in Gasparilla village. In 1908, Gus Cole, a commercial fisherman, and his wife and oldest daughter built their home on a small island (Cole Island) just to the north of Gasparilla Island. The Jones Fishery moved from Placida to Gasparilla village in 1907–1908 and, in 1910, a post office was established (the village was now a flag stop of the railroad). It became the policy of the CH&N to encourage the growth of the fishing village so that the railroad could use its freight capacity to ship iced fish by rail to distribution points on the mainland. Moreover, the village was becoming a growing market for goods shipped by train. Thus, in 1914, the railroad built two icehouses on the east side of a siding located just to the north of the post office and, in 1916, arranged for construction of 16 new houses leased to fishermen in the village. Between 1914 and 1945, Gasparilla prospered, developing a population of about 60 inhabitants.

In the 1940s, refrigerated trucks gradually took over much of the job of delivering iced fish to urban markets. In addition, Port Tampa began to displace Boca Grande as the preferred terminal from which to export phosphate. In December 1945, the American Agricultural Chemical Company (AACCo), which had built Port Boca Grande and the railroad to Gasparilla Island, sold all its remaining land, including the village of Gasparilla, to Sunset Realty Inc. It was generally recognized that Sunset planned to replace the fishing village with an upscale real estate development. In anticipation of Gasparilla's inevitable demise, most of its residents moved away.

By the early 1950s, almost all of Gasparilla's inhabitants had left and this once dynamic village took on an abandoned appearance. It was soon bulldozed out of existence, and today condominiums stand on the site of the once flourishing village. Commercial fishing, however, continued to be the livelihood of hundreds of families in the harbor area for several more decades. In 1985, Charlotte Harbor was noted as a major center of the U.S. commercial mullet fishery. More than 24 million pounds of the fish were being harvested annually. Mullet in huge numbers were caught in Charlotte Harbor until 1995, when a constitutional amendment was passed in Florida banning large nets in inshore waters. Sport fishing, too, was on the rise as the 20th century progressed. Charlotte Harbor's fishing began to attract anglers in search of recreation, and commercial fishermen would turn to charter fishing. The members of the Boca Grande Fishing Guides Association, and today's multi-million dollar sportfishing industry in Charlotte Harbor, are the inheritors of Charlotte Harbor's time-honored fishing tradition.

In this c. 1901 portrait of members of the Padilla fishing community of Cayo Costa are patriarch Tariva Padilla (just to the left of center with the white beard) and his wife, Juanita, at his right. (Courtesy of Robert F. Edic.)

Gasparilla Village's fish houses sit along the railroad right-of-way in this c. 1918 view looking south from the railroad trestle. (Courtesy of Robert F. Edic.)

Walter Gault was the founder of the wholesale fish business in Placida and the proprietor of Gasparilla's last remaining fish house. (Courtesy of Eunice Gault Albritton.)

Fish caught by local fishermen were delivered to two fish houses in Gasparilla where they were kept on ice and transferred daily to insulated boxcars for shipment to northern markets. Initially, the ice came from Cedar Key; later, it came from Arcadia and was delivered to Gasparilla by rail. (Courtesy of Robert F. Edic.)

A CH&N locomotive is shown stopping at Gasparilla, c. 1920. The village's two icehouses are visible on the right. (Courtesy of Robert F. Edic.)

Albert Lowe, one of Gasparilla's fishermen, is pictured with a nice catch of mullet. (Courtesy of the *Boca Beacon*.)

An engine on the main track and a box car on the side track, as well as some of the villagers, are seen in this photo of Gasparilla.

A train arrives at Gasparilla Village from Boca Grande. The IGA general store is visible on pilings at the left. The train came through Gasparilla every day, bringing ice and supplies and picking up both fish and passengers. (Courtesy of Robert F. Edic.)

Children of the Gasparilla school pose with their teacher John Fish in 1923–1924. (Courtesy of the *Boca Beacon*.)

Fishing was hard work. Besides setting the nets, hauling in the fish, and spreading the nets to dry, fishermen were constantly mending nets, as they are doing here in Gasparilla about 1926. (Courtesy of Eunice Gault Albritton.)

A mullet net is visible in the stern of this fishing skiff off Cayo Costa about 1910. (Courtesy of Robert F. Edic.)

The "run boat" *Ray* makes a routine stop at the Punta Blanca ice station. The *Ray* was one of two regular run boats maintained by the Punta Gorda Fish Company (the other was the *Harris Brothers*). The Punta Gorda Fish Company was founded in 1897 by E.C. Knight, together with L.B. Giddens. Every two days, these boats delivered ice to the harbor's ice stations and picked up the freshly caught fish that had been left at the icehouses by independent fishermen. The last captain to operate a run boat in Charlotte Harbor was Walter "Homer" Monson (the grandson of E.C. Knight), who made the final run in June 1959. (Courtesy of Robert F. Edic.)

Capt. Alfonso Darna delivers a load of mullet, still in the nets, to the Punta Blanca ice station just south of Boca Grande Pass about 1938. Adjoining the icehouse (at left) is a small bunkhouse for fishermen. This fish house and two others were burned to the water by unknown persons following the Florida ban on inshore netting with large nets in 1995. (Courtesy of the Boca Grande Historical Society.)

Nets dry in the sun at Gasparilla in the early 1950s. (Courtesy of the *Boca Beacon* and Dr. Dennis Dorsey.)

Abandoned Gasparilla fish houses in the 1950s are visible in this view looking north. In 1945, Walter Gault, Gasparilla's last fish house proprietor, moved his operation to Placida on the mainland at the northern end of the railroad trestle. It seems likely that this move was related to American Agricultural Chemical Co.'s 1945 sale of the northern end of the island, including the village of Gasparilla, to Sunset Realty Corporation. (Courtesy of the Boca Grande Historical Society.)

The icehouses in Charlotte Harbor remained in use until the early 1950s. Several still survive and are in private hands. Most of them have been placed on the National Register of Historic Places. (Courtesy of the *Boca Beacon*.)

Two

Two Lighthouses

The Boca Grande Lighthouse

The Port Boca Grande Lighthouse—originally called the Gasparilla Island Light Station—was built in 1890 at the southern tip of Gasparilla Island on the southwest coast to mark the entry into Charlotte Harbor from the Gulf of Mexico. From its perch on deep water Boca Grande Pass, it first saw service guiding cattle ships going from Charlotte Harbor to Cuba, as well as ships coming to load phosphate ore, which was transported down the Peace River on barges. In 1912, Port Boca Grande, served by a railroad from the phosphate mines in Polk County, opened as a state-of-the art international shipping facility. For the next 67 years, the lighthouse, with its 3.5-order Fresnel lens, helped guide ocean-going ships from more than 20 countries coming to Boca Grande to load phosphate, a valuable commodity worldwide for making fertilizer.

The lighthouse, now known simply as the Boca Grande Lighthouse, is the oldest building on Gasparilla Island. The assistant lightkeeper's house next door, of nearly identical style but without the lantern tower, was built at the same time. The restored buildings are today the centerpiece of Gasparilla Island State Recreation Area.

In 1890, except for the small fishing camp on Peacon's Cove at the north end of the island, the only buildings on Gasparilla Island were the lighthouse, the assistant lightkeeper's house, and a pilot station. But by 1905, the railroad was on its way, and by 1912, the port of Boca Grande was in operation. The keepers of the lighthouse who lived and worked in the building, often with their families, were: Francis McNulty, 1890–1894; William Lester, 1894–1923; Charles Henry Williams, 1923–1932; Osmund M. McKinney, 1932–1940; and Cody W. McKeithen 1941–1951. During most of these years there was an assistant keeper living in the building next door.

The lighthouse—a one-story wooden bungalow on iron pilings with a black octagonal lantern tower on top—has survived seven hurricanes, a fire that burned down a washhouse just a few feet away, and severe beach erosion. In the early years, lighthouse keepers, living a lonely life on the isolated barrier island, played host to millionaires like John D. Rockefeller and John Jacob Astor, who came to Boca Grande Pass in their yachts to fish for the mighty tarpon. During World War II, the light guided hundreds of grateful U.S. and Allied cargo ships, seeking refuge from German submarines off the coast, into safe harborage.

The lighthouse keeper had to be eternally vigilant. His most important tasks were to make sure the kerosene lamp (later, oil was used) inside the lens didn't go out, and to make sure the powerful Fresnel magnifying lens revolved all night long. The lens was a "fixed white light of 3 1/2 power with a red flash every 20 seconds" (U.S. Army Office of the Lighthouse Engineer, 1889). It revolved by means of a clockwork-type mechanism powered by a heavy weight, similar to a "grandfather's clock." The weight had to be reset every two hours. In the ceiling, one can still see the hole through which the weight, on ropes or chains, dropped as the mechanism unwound. The keeper had to keep the light in good working order. This entailed polishing the lens, cleaning and filling the lamp, and trimming the wicks. He also was responsible for maintaining the building and the grounds and had to keep a log of his activities and the goings-on at the lighthouse. After 1927, when the tall "Rear Range Light" was installed a mile up the road, he had to tend to that lighthouse as well. All of these tasks created an unending round of daily chores that required stamina, skill, patience, and dedication.

In 1956, the lighthouse was automated and left unmanned, and in 1966, the light was removed and the Coast Guard turned the building over to the federal General Services Administration for disposal. Thirteen acres of land and the ownership of the dilapidated building—leaning at an angle, with stairs rotted away and Gulf waters lapping at it owing to beach erosion—were transferred to Lee County in 1972. The local power company, Florida Power and Light, helped the lighthouse survive by pumping sand around the building and building two rock groins along the new shoreline.

The lighthouse was placed on the National Register of Historic Places in 1980, and in 1985–1986, island citizens, under the leadership of the Gasparilla Island Conservation and Improvement Association, restored the lighthouse with help from the Florida Bureau of Historic Preservation. A 377-mm drum lens was installed, and the lighthouse was re-commissioned by the Coast Guard on November 21, 1986. The State of Florida took over ownership in 1988, and in 1999, the lighthouse opened to the public as the Boca Grande Lighthouse Museum. The museum was created and is operated by the Barrier Island Parks Society, a volunteer organization for the park. The Coast Guard maintains the light, which continues to mark the southern tip of Gasparilla Island as it has done since 1890.

The Boca Grande Lighthouse came precariously close to total destruction; its life was renewed and it is open to the public today through a remarkable effort of government, citizens, and businesses working together to preserve an important piece of Florida's history.

The Boca Grande Entrance Rear Range Light

The Boca Grande Entrance Rear Range Light—on the Gulf about a mile north of the Port Boca Grande Lighthouse—is one of only a handful of lighthouses that have had active service in two states. According to new research by lighthouse historians, this lighthouse was originally built in 1881 to serve as the Delaware Breakwater Rear Range Lighthouse, north of Lewes, Delaware, and was known locally as the Green Hill Lighthouse. In 1918, owing to shoreline changes, the lighthouse was discontinued, and its lens and clockwork were shipped for use on the west coast of the United States.

In 1919, the Seventh Lighthouse District in Florida notified the district supervisor in Delaware that they had need for the tower in Florida. In 1921, the lighthouse tower was dismantled, each part being numbered for easy re-assembly, and shipped by railroad to Miami. Funding problems delayed the erection of the "Green Hill Lighthouse" on Gasparilla Island, but in 1927, the United States Lighthouse Service erected the skeletal, 105-foot-tall Rear Range Light on the beach just south of the village of Boca Grande. It seems to have taken some years to procure a lens for the tower; current research indicates that the lens was not lit until 1932. The light was never manned and was maintained by the keepers of the Boca Grande Lighthouse. It was of great commercial importance during the hey-day of Port Boca Grande in the third quarter of the century, guiding ships from all over the world through the treacherous waters of the Boca Grande Navigation Channel into safe harborage inside Charlotte Harbor.

It is the Rear Range Light that is mainly used to help vessels safely enter Port Boca Grande. The captain can tell which of the two Boca Grande lighthouses he is seeing because of the difference in the flash sequences. As a vessel proceeds in the ship's channel, heading for south Gasparilla Island, the captain sees, fixed in the water, the Front Range Light, a 20-foot-tall steel structure with a flashing light on top. He lines up this range light with the tall Rear Range Light on land. By so doing, he knows he is in the middle of the ship's channel.

At this time, the future of the Boca Grande Entrance Rear Range Light is uncertain. In 1998, Florida Power and Light, the sole commercial user of Port Boca Grande, announced that by 2002 it will no longer need or use the Port Boca Grande oil terminal to receive oil shipments; and in August 1999, the Coast Guard announced that it was turning the Rear Range Light over to the federal General Services Administration.

In 1888, the U.S. Congress appropriated $35,000 to the United States Lighthouse Service to build the "Gasparilla Island Light Station" at the south end of Gasparilla Island. The light was lit on December 31, 1890. On the steps of this 1890 photograph is Capt. Peter Nelsen, one of the first three harbor pilots of Port Boca Grande. (Courtesy of the Boca Grande Lighthouse Museum.)

This unusual c. 1912 view, looking towards the west at the east sides of the lighthouse and assistant keeper's house, foreshortens the distance between the two buildings. (Courtesy of the Florida State Archives.)

This c. 1915 image shows the assistant lightkeeper's house. Note the walkway and privy. In the background is one of Port Boca Grande's large phosphate "dry bins," the 1,000-foot-long phosphate dock, and a ship. (Courtesy of the Gasparilla Inn.)

Lighthouse keeper Charles Henry Williams poses with Melva and Elva Tucker on the wharf in front of the lighthouse, c. 1925. (Courtesy of the family of Charles Henry Williams.)

Lighthouse keeper Osmund McKinney is pictured here with his wife, Lois, and children Ruth, Calvin, and Evelyn on the steps of the lighthouse in 1938. (Courtesy of Evelyn McKinney Ferguson.)

The McKinney children are on the wharf in front of the lighthouse. (Courtesy of Evelyn McKinney Ferguson.)

Shortly after this picture was taken, probably in 1939, the "wash house" between the two buildings burned to the ground when Ruth McKinney, the young daughter of lighthouse keeper Osmund McKinney, accidentally started a fire. Nearby port workers ran over to help put out the fire and save the lighthouse. (Courtesy of the Boca Grande Lighthouse Museum.)

The wharf, or pier, which had been in place since before 1910, became a "hazard" by 1960, according to the U.S. Coast Guard, and was torn down shortly thereafter. Note the two wooden water cisterns next to the assistant keeper's house. These can still be seen today. (Courtesy of the Boca Grande Lighthouse Museum.)

In 1966, the U.S. Coast Guard determined that the lighthouse was no longer needed. The light was removed, and the Coast Guard turned the building over to the federal General Services Administration for disposal. The stairs rotted away and the old building grew more dilapidated with each passing year. By 1970, the sea had swept away the sand around the lighthouse until it was standing in the water. Soon the seaward side of the building started to sink. (Courtesy of the Boca Grande Lighthouse Museum.)

In another view of the lighthouse standing in the water, the cisterns are visible underneath the building. (Courtesy of the Robert W. Johnson family.)

In 1972, Lee County took over ownership of the lighthouse and the surrounding 13 acres from the federal government. The county used funds from the sale of a small unused piece of property on the island to straighten the tilt of the lighthouse. Also in 1972, Florida Power and Light (FPL), which owns the oil terminal next door, dredged the basin at its dock and placed 35,000 cubic yards of sand around the building. Two rock groins, seen in this photograph, were placed along the new shoreline to help hold the sand in place. (Courtesy of the Boca Grande Lighthouse Museum.)

The lighthouse was placed on the National Register of Historic Places in 1980, but the building continued to deteriorate. It is seen here just prior to the start of restoration work in 1985. (Courtesy of the Boca Grande Lighthouse Museum.)

The Boca Grande Lighthouse is today the centerpiece of Gasparilla Island State Park. The assistant keeper's house is the park headquarters. (Courtesy of the Boca Grande Lighthouse Museum.)

The Boca Grande Entrance Rear Range Light, on the beach about a mile north of the old lighthouse, is known locally as the Coast Guard Range Light, or simply, the "range light." This c. 1950 picture of the lighthouse shows the old Boca Grande Hotel in the upper right and the Boca Grande School (today the community center) behind the hotel. (Courtesy of Florida State Archives.)

The Coast Guard Range Light still stands tall on the beach, but its future is uncertain. (Courtesy of Florida State Archives.)

Three
Phosphate, the Railroad, and Port Boca Grande

In 1881, a discovery was made that would change the character of Gasparilla Island forever. Phosphate, in great demand worldwide for use in the production of fertilizer, was discovered in the Peace River Valley to the northeast of Boca Grande. It was this discovery that would bring the railroad to Gasparilla Island and would result in the construction of both the port and the town of Boca Grande.

"River pebble" phosphate was first mined in the Peace River near Arcadia and Zolfo Springs in 1888. "Land pebble" mining began in 1890, and by 1900, land mining had replaced river mining. The river valley itself became known as "Bone Valley" because of the thousands of bones and fossilized remains of mastodons and other prehistoric animals found in association with the phosphate deposits. The industry soon spread the length of the Peace River Valley, centering around Mulberry and Bartow.

In the early years of the industry, after the phosphate rock was mined, washed, dried, sorted, and ground, it was brought to the Gulf of Mexico for shipment by two methods—rail and barge. At first it was transported by rail to Porta Gorda on the east side of Charlotte Harbor. But, in 1897, the rails to the "Long Dock" in Punta Gorda were removed, and rail shipment of phosphate to Punta Gorda ceased. Far more commonly, phosphate was transported down the Peace River to Charlotte Harbor in barges, where it was transferred onto ocean-going ships near the deep water of Boca Grande Pass (the channel between Charlotte Harbor and the Gulf of Mexico) at the southern tip of Gasparilla Island.

In the late 1890s, the newly created American Agricultural Chemical Company (AACCo), controlled by the Bradleys of the Bradley Fertilizer Works near Boston, acquired land containing extensive deposits of high-grade phosphate in the Peace River Valley. By 1904, the company had decided to build a rail line from the phosphate mines to the deep water of Boca Grande Pass in order to expedite shipping and meet growing competition in the industry. There were six buildings—three small port buildings, the lighthouse, the assistant lightkeeper's cottage, and a quarantine station—at the southern tip of Gasparilla Island in February 1905, when an AACCo company official, an engineer from the U.S. Engineering Corps, and a work force of at least 30 laborers landed on the island. They set up tents, and the surveying and construction of the new railroad branch north and eastward to the mines began.

The railway began at the southern tip of the island, passed through the island's 7-mile length, and crossed the upper reaches of the harbor (Gasparilla Sound) and the Myakka River on trestles. It continued 40 miles overland to Arcadia, crossing the Peace River on a bridge nearly a mile long. There were 90 trestles on the railroad utilizing more than 3 miles of lumber. More than 2 miles of trestlework plus two separate drawbridges were needed for the crossing of Gasparilla Sound. The tracks were laid with 70-pound steel rail with the use of earth ballast.

While work was commencing from Boca Grande, construction was also proceeding on the mainland. The Charlotte Harbor and Northern Railway, a subsidiary of the American Agricultural Chemical Company, was completed from Port Boca Grande to Arcadia on June 30, 1907. In 1910, the line was completed to a connection with the Seaboard Air Line Railway at Bradley Junction. It also was extended to the phosphate mines around Mulberry, to a connection with the Atlantic Coast Line Railroad.

By 1911, AACCo had built a fully automated phosphate loading facility at Port Boca Grande—the first of its kind in the United States. For 20 years, large sailing ships and steamships had been loading phosphate from barges inside Charlotte Harbor. Now phosphate could be shipped directly by rail from the mines in Polk County to Boca Grande Pass. In 1912, the first cargo ship was loaded from the new 1,000-foot dock extending out into deep water.

Soon the port (known as "South Dock" to the locals) would become a bustling community. Port and railroad workers, both white and African American, lived there with their families, as did the quarantine doctor, the lighthouse keeper and assistant lightkeeper and their families, and the harbor pilots and their families. There was a separate school for black children that provided grades one through six.

Port Boca Grande was important for another reason during the early years of World War II. As a deep-water port on the Gulf of Mexico, it was used for the shipment of supplies to the European Allies in the early days of the war. Tons of ammunition and dynamite were loaded into British and Allied ships and taken, via Key West, across the Atlantic to Europe. In addition, thousands of underwater mines assembled in Placida on the mainland were loaded at the port for defense against German submarines ("U-boats") in the Gulf of Mexico.

After the United States entered the war in 1941, the port offered a safe refuge at night for cargo ships. German submarines lurked off all parts of Florida's Atlantic and Gulf coasts during the early years of the war. During the summer of 1942, more than 100 Allied ships were sunk in the Gulf of Mexico. Cargo ships leaving Houston, New Orleans, and other Gulf ports were ordered by the Navy to anchor at night at any available port. The deep-water port and anchorage of Boca Grande, having pilot service, became an important point of refuge along the Gulf coast.

Activities at Port Boca Grande reached their hey-day in the 1960s and early 1970s. Not only was the phosphate business thriving, the electric company that provides power to all of Southwest Florida, Florida Power and Light, built its own dock and storage facility in 1958. Now Boca Grande was a two-terminal port.

Between 200 and 250 ships from all over the world were coming into the port each year. Ships' crews of all nationalities visited the village of Boca Grande at mid-island to shop, eat, drink, and socialize. Port officials entertained officers and captains of the ships in their homes, and sometimes dined with them aboard their ships. There was much social interaction between the men of the ships and the inhabitants of the island. At its peak, Port Boca Grande covered 40 acres and employed about 60 people. In 1969, Port Boca Grande ranked fourth in the state of Florida in tonnage handled.

The rail lines from the Peace River Valley to Port Boca Grande and to Tampa made Florida's immense phosphate industry possible. The industry in Florida today employs more than 10,000 people. It produces about 85 percent of the U.S phosphate supply and about 35 percent of the world market. In the 1970s, phosphate companies increasingly switched their interests to ports in Tampa and Manatee County, where larger amounts of phosphate could be handled more efficiently than at the aging Port Boca Grande. The port began to dwindle, and in 1979, the last load of phosphate left Charlotte Harbor aboard a Japanese ship bound for Japan.

Florida Power and Light continued to use Port Boca Grande as an oil storage facility until the fall of 2001, when that use also came to an end. For 43 years oil-laden tankers and barges from across the Gulf of Mexico had brought oil to the port, where it was off-loaded into four large storage tanks and then transported down the Intracoastal Waterway to FPL's Fort Myers power plant. The conversion of FPL's generating plant from oil to natural gas, completed in 2001, brought its need for oil to an end, and brought an end to Port Boca Grande as well

Foreign ships that came to Port Boca Grande were quarantined until their crews were given a clean bill of health by a state-employed "quarantine doctor." The first quarantine station was built at the south end of the Gasparilla Island in 1895. This photo shows it nearly 100 years later, in about 1990, prior to its being enlarged and renovated in 1995. After the government built a new quarantine station in 1904, across Boca Grande Pass at north Cayo Costa, this building became the pilot station. Note the "widow's walk" at the top. It was moved about 200 yards to the northwest in the 1920s. (Courtesy of the *Boca Beacon*.)

The "new" quarantine station was built by the federal government at the north end of Cayo Costa in 1904 and served the port until about 1925. It was about 100 yards from shore, connected to the beach by a walkway on pilings. The doctor kept his boat in a slip under the house. Before the railroad and post office came to Port Boca Grande, mail and telegraph communications were delivered to this station by the passenger steamer from Punta Gorda en route to Fort Myers. (Courtesy of the Charlotte Harbor Area Historical Society.)

On November 28, 1905, the steamboat *Mistletoe* carried AACCo official L.M. Fouts, his son Edwin, a civil engineer, and a crew of dozens of laborers from Tampa to Gasparilla Island to begin work on the railroad. They landed on the Gulf side of the island not far from what is now the "range light" public beach. The *Mistletoe*, owned by John Savarese, first began to provide transportation for the Sarasota Bay area in 1895. (Courtesy of Sarasota County Historical Resources.)

The tent encampment of the railroad construction crew seen here was located at the south end of Gasparilla Island in 1905. (Courtesy of the Charlotte Harbor Area Historical Society.)

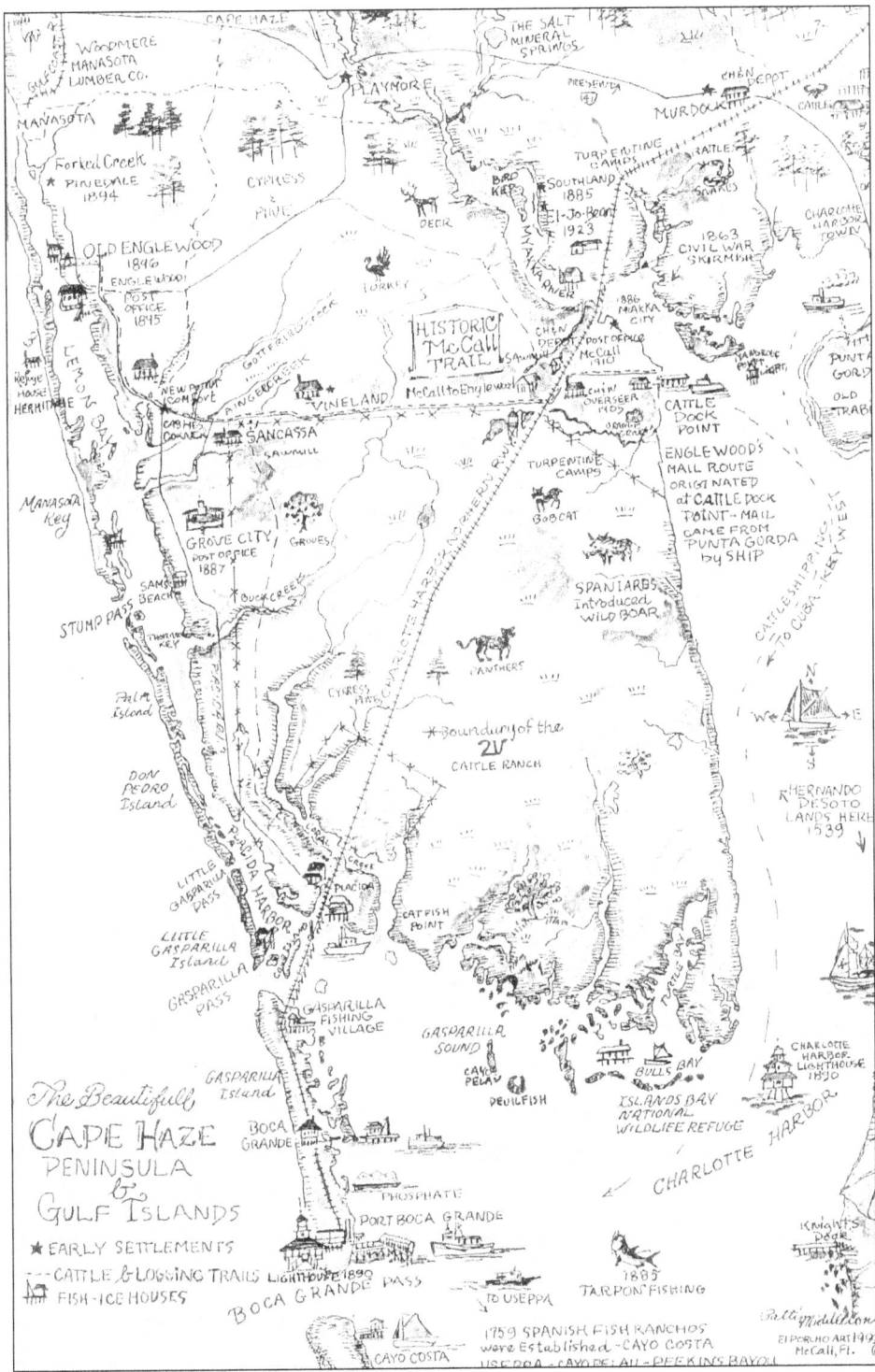

This map of the Cape Haze Peninsula and the barrier islands shows the route of the Charlotte Harbor and Northern rail line across the Myakka River and the peninsula, and down the length of Gasparilla Island to Port Boca Grande. (Map created by and courtesy of Patti Middleton.)

The conveyor belt system is under construction at the phosphate dock in this c. 1911 image. (Courtesy of the Charlotte Harbor Area Historical Society.)

The CH&N railroad was known among some of its workers as the "Cold, Hungry and Naked," a nickname coined by them after Robert Bradley took over control of the line. Evidently, Bradley's efforts to cut costs engendered less than enthusiastic admiration among the railroad workers. Seen here is a c. 1924 Charlotte Harbor and Northern engine. (Courtesy of the *Boca Beacon*.)

Two huge phosphate "dry bins" dominated the port landscape; one is shown here, c. 1915. (Courtesy of the Charlotte Harbor Area Historical Society.)

A CH&N locomotive is shown at the port, c. 1920s. The man on the right holding the shovel is probably the fireman. (Courtesy of the Charlotte Harbor Area Historical Society.)

Trainsmen at the port were kept busy switching phosphate cars. (Courtesy of the Charlotte Harbor Area Historical Society.)

Seaboard Air Line Railway purchased the CH&N Railroad for $22.5 million in 1925 and took over the "Boca Grande route." The name Seaboard would gradually replace the old CH&N on the trains. CSX Corporation, successors to Seaboard Air Line Railway, created Gasparilla Island's "Boca Bay" development beginning in the 1980s.

The power plant for Port Boca Grande, known today as the "powerhouse," was built by the American Agricultural Chemical Company in 1909 to provide electricity for the port. It soon provided power for all of Boca Grande in a day when most communities on the mainland did not yet have power. For 42 years, Boca Grande depended on the powerhouse for electricity. In 1952, Florida Power and Light was granted the franchise to provide power to Gasparilla Island, and the old plant was shut down. This photograph shows the abandoned powerhouse in the 1970s, prior to its restoration. (Courtesy of the *Boca Beacon*.)

In the early days of the port, many of the vessels that came to Port Boca Grande to load phosphate were four- or five-masted schooners. These "Yankee" ships took phosphate back to states from Delaware to Maine. By 1920, steamships had completely replaced sailing vessels. The pier in the foreground of this *c.* 1915 photograph, known as the lumber dock, was torn down in the late 1920s. (Courtesy of the Charlotte Harbor Area Historical Society.)

This c. 1915 view of the port looks northwest towards the powerhouse, which is just to the left of center. (Courtesy of the Charlotte Harbor Area Historical Society.)

The port's phosphate "sampling tower" is seen here just to the right of center. Farther to the right is one of the two enormous warehouses, or "dry bins." (Courtesy of the Charlotte Harbor Area Historical Society.)

A switch engine positions phosphate cars at the dumping station, where phosphate rock was loaded onto a conveyor belt system and transferred the length of the dock to waiting ships. The system, with 17,000 feet of conveyor belt, could move 16 tons of phosphate per minute. The huge bins could hold 37,800 tons of phosphate. (Courtesy of the Charlotte Harbor Area Historical Society.)

This view shows phosphate cars and a switch engine at the port. During the port's peak years, trains up to 100 cars long arrived daily with their loads of phosphate ore. (Courtesy of the Charlotte Harbor Area Historical Society.)

Phosphate was unloaded from rail cars onto the conveyor belt, which took it aloft into the huge bin at the right. Ten thousand tons of phosphate rock could be loaded on a ship within 15 hours at Port Boca Grande, according to a 1950 booklet on Lee County published by a Fort Myers bank. (Courtesy of the Charlotte Harbor Area Historical Society.)

The phosphate dock extended 1,000 feet out into the waters of Charlotte Harbor, just inside Boca Grande Pass. At first, trains took the phosphate out to the waiting ships, where cranes and elevators above the dock dumped it into the ships' holds. (Courtesy of the *Boca Beacon*.)

The combination "depot" and general store at the port was run by Capt. Kingsmore Johnson Sr., seen here c. 1920s. (Courtesy of the Charlotte Harbor Area Historical Society.)

Jefferson Gaines Sr. has hooked into a big fish with a cane pole. He is near the pilot boat dock; note the phosphate dock in the background of this c. 1930 image. (Courtesy of Jeff Gaines.)

This aerial view of the phosphate dock shows its imposing size, c. 1940. (Courtesy of the Boca Grande Historical Society.)

A power boat speeds by the phosphate dock in this c. 1965 view from inside the harbor. (Courtesy of the *Boca Beacon*.)

The superstructure of the dock was removed by CSX Corp. in the early 1990s, and the decking was removed in 1999–2000. All that remains of the dock today are the pilings. (Courtesy of the *Boca Beacon*.)

By the time this bird's-eye view of Port Boca Grande was made c. 1950, the port covered 40 acres and employed between 50 and 60 people, "none of whom earns less than $200 per month" according to a 1950 Lee County promotional booklet. (Courtesy of the *Boca Beacon*.)

Ships from more than 20 countries came to Port Boca Grande during the 1950s, 1960s, and 1970s to load phosphate and take it all over the world. This is a steam freighter, c. 1955. (Courtesy of the Robert W. Johnson family.)

An average of 10 to 12 ships per month, like this large freighter, each carrying about 10,000 long tons of phosphate, left the port for all parts of the globe. These ships earned approximately $50,000 per cargo. (Courtesy of the Robert W. Johnson family.)

In 1947, 730,452 tons of phosphate were shipped from Port Boca Grande. By the 1960s, about 100,000 tons of phosphate a month were being shipped. The largest ship ever accommodated at the port—the *Buntentor* out of Germany (not pictured)—was 750 feet long. The deepest ship had a draft of 31 feet, 10 inches. (Courtesy of the Robert W. Johnson family.)

This aerial view of the south end, taken in the early 1960s, has several interesting features. It shows the first oil storage tank built by Florida Power and Light just a few years earlier, as well as the new "oil dock" in front of it. (The phosphate dock is at upper left.) The photo also shows "Tarpon Pass Estates" (two rows of houses in front of the oil tank), where African Americans who worked at the port and elsewhere on the island lived from the late 1950s until 1983. The L-shaped pier in the foreground is a fishing pier, the landward end of which was damaged in a hurricane in 1960. Note the lighthouse at the extreme tip (far right) of the island. (Courtesy of the Boca Grande Lighthouse Museum.)

A c. early 1960s aerial view of Gasparilla Island clearly shows the railroad tracks running the length of the island. Note how the tracks, when they reach the port, split into two directions, eastward and westward. This "triangulation"—called a wye—permitted engines to turn around. Note the tanker unloading oil at the oil dock. (Courtesy of the Florida State Archives.)

By the time this c. 1970 photograph of Port Boca Grande was taken, Florida Power and Light Co. had added another oil tank to its storage terminal. Note the freighter loading phosphate at the phosphate dock. (Courtesy of the Florida State Archives.)

Capt. Iredell W. Johnson was a Port Boca Grande harbor pilot from 1888 to 1933. He and his brother, Capt. William H. Johnson, were the first pilots at the port. A short time later, they were joined by Capt. Peter Nelsen. All three had been large vessel captains and pilots out of the port of Punta Gorda. They were the first permanent settlers of South Boca Grande. (Courtesy of the Robert W. Johnson family.)

Capt. Peter Nelsen was a harbor pilot from 1888 to 1906. He also founded the town of Alva near Fort Myers, was a Lee County commissioner, and was postmaster of Cayo Costa. Captain Nelsen spent the last part of his life on Cayo Costa island, where he built a school and is buried. (Courtesy of Charles Foster.)

The *Comet* (at left) served as the Boca Grande pilot boat for about 30 years beginning in 1911. She was 40 feet long, 8 feet wide, built of cypress, and initially powered with a three-cylinder, 18-horsepower gasoline engine. She could run out to the sea buoy, a distance of 5 miles, in about 30 minutes. (Courtesy of the Robert W. Johnson family.)

The *Pilot* served as the Boca Grande pilot boat from 1939 until 1974. The pilots met incoming ships at sea in their small boats, climbed aboard, took control of the helm, and piloted the vessels into safe port. (Courtesy of the *Boca Beacon*.)

This "new" *Pilot* replaced the old *Pilot* in 1974. (Courtesy of the *Boca Beacon*.)

The mixing and mingling of ships' crews, pilots and their families, townfolk, and port workers resulted in many "international" acquaintances and friendships during the years of Port Boca Grande's hey-day. This is the crew of the *Tresca*, a large sailing sloop out of England by way of Bermuda, which ended up at the port during a storm in the early 1950s. Little Roseanne, at far right with her father, the ship's mechanic and engineer, became the "darling of the port" for ten days while the *Tresca* underwent engine, hull, and sail repairs. (Courtesy of the Robert W. Johnson family.)

A view looking east shows the Amory Memorial Chapel in relation to the lighthouse and one of Florida

An aerial view of the island, c. 1990, shows many changes at the south end: Gone are the port buildings; the railroad bed has been transformed into the island's bicycle path; the oil terminal now has four storage tanks; and development of the upscale housing development Boca Bay is evident. (Courtesy of Dusty Hopkins.)

Power and Light's oil tanks. (Courtesy of the Boca Grande Lighthouse Museum.)

The Shiloh Baptist Church (known today as the Amory Memorial Chapel), near the lighthouse, was built for the community of African Americans at the south end by Roger and Louise Amory in 1959. The Amorys also built and endowed the Johann Fust Community Library in Boca Grande, and the library owned the church until 1986. In that year, the library donated the church to the Gasparilla Island Conservation and Improvement Association (GICIA). In 1987, the GICIA gave the building to the state of Florida and it became part of Gasparilla Island State Park. In 1996, the chapel was restored with funds from the GICIA, the Boca Grande Woman's Club, the Lee County Historic Preservation Board, and the Venice Foundation. (Courtesy of the Boca Grande Lighthouse Museum.)

The old quarantine house is pictured here following its 1995 renovation and enlargement. It is the oldest house on the island and is listed on the National Register of Historic Places. Five generations of Johnsons, the harbor pilot family, have lived in the house. (Courtesy of the Boca Grande Lighthouse Museum.)

In 1995, the old powerhouse was restored by CSX Corporation and placed on the National Register of Historic Places. Today it is a social center and meeting place for the residents of CSX's Boca Bay development and a place for selected community events. (Courtesy of the *Boca Beacon*.)

Four

Boca Grande: A Unique Island Town

Boca Grande existed on paper long before it became a town in actuality. In January 1897, Albert W. Gilchrist, an engineer and surveyor from Punta Gorda (later to become governor of Florida), filed a plat with Lee County encompassing six blocks along the Gulf of Mexico just to the north of the 2-mile-long federally owned military reserve at Gasparilla's south end. On this plat, three blocks were on the Gulf and three were situated to the west, separated by a street unabashedly called Gilchrist Avenue. The cross streets were named First, Second, Third, and Fourth Streets. This platted area, which Gilchrist named "Town of Boca Grande on Gasparilla Island," was placed at the widest part of the island and was therefore well suited for residential development. However, for more than a decade, the streets were not actually laid out and no lots were sold.

In 1907, Peter Bradley, the president of AACCo, and a senior associate, attorney James M. Gifford, took a careful look at Gilchrist's plat. As AACCo's historian, Anthony B. Arnold, put it, "Perhaps it was this plat, or maybe it was the lovely beach with sunshine sparkling on the Gulf with pelicans wheeling above that inspired Mr. Gifford and Mr. Bradley with the idea of developing Gasparilla as a high class winter resort. Jekyll Island, Georgia, had been developed as a millionaire's club. Railroad pioneers had built sumptuous hotels on their lines to attract passengers and prospective home builders to the town sites along their routes . . . Why should not the Charlotte Harbor & Northern Railway (CH&N) follow suit? Straightway, Mr. Gifford and Mr. Bradley became the first directors of the Boca Grande Land Company, chartered by the State of Florida on April 29, 1907, to buy, sell and develop real estate . . . It was proposed to buy all the land on Gasparilla Island north of the Military Reserve then held by Gilchrist and his partner, John P. Wall, for $100,000 . . . The officers were authorized to file a new plat . . . (that) showed a wide street called Gulf Boulevard between the front of the Gulf lots and the bank at the top of the beach . . . Thus, the real estate business was launched with AACCo money furnished through the Peace River Mining Company, and was operated by employees of the CH&N."

On February 21, 1909, a meeting was held at the Useppa Inn at which it was decided to build a resort hotel on Gasparilla Island. The plans for the Inn, prepared by Augustus D. Shepherd, were approved, and construction on the hotel was begun in 1910. When the 20-room "Hotel Boca Grande" (as it was called initially) was completed in time for the 1911–1912 season, it was already too small. Hence, in October 1912, the Boca Grande Land Company borrowed money from the CH&N to double the Inn's size and furnish it. Karl Abbott, the first manager of the Gasparilla Inn (the name was changed from Hotel Boca Grande by 1913) was so successful in attracting an upscale clientele to the Inn that, late in 1915, $85,000 was allocated to double its size once again and to build servant quarters on the Inn's grounds. Francis J. Kennard of Tampa, who had designed the first enlargement in 1912, was also the architect of the second, and ensured that the project would be completed in time for the 1916–1917 season.

In August 1907, CH&N was ready to begin operation between Arcadia and Boca Grande, and in that year, a small wooden-frame depot was built at the intersection of Park and Fourth Streets, in the center of the new town of Boca Grande. In 1909, this depot was replaced by a much larger brick structure of Mediterranean Revival design. The depot served as headquarters for CH&N, with railway offices on the second floor, and a waiting room and ticket office on the first floor. A few years later, when the depot was enlarged, a telegraph office was added, together with offices for CH&N's phosphate operations.

As the town of Boca Grande grew, it acquired a number of businesses, including two grocery stores, a "drug store" which was also a general store (Fugate's), a bank, a telephone exchange, a mini-department store (the "Mercantile"), several dress shops, a flower shop, a movie theater, several small inns, an ice storage house, a car dealership and gas station, several marinas, and a fish market. Ultimately, there were four churches (Baptist, Episcopalian, Methodist, and Roman Catholic) in downtown Boca Grande. There was also a Community House (used by the residents for parties, receptions, meetings, and other events), and a medical clinic. There was also a school for grades one through twelve.

The growing town attracted entrepreneurs of all kinds. Some worked for the railroad, some came to start their own businesses. Some of the business and civic leaders of the early community, all of whom came to the town prior to 1920, were Jerome Fugate Sr., Jefferson Gaines Sr., Arthur Guerard, George Knight, Richard Kuhl, W.C. McCranie, William Riley Polk, T. Holloway, John E. Riley, Sam Whidden, and Fred Thompson. Descendants of many of these men still reside in Boca Grande today.

In 1921, major changes occurred in AACCo's management. Peter Bradley, by then 71 years of age, resigned as president of the company. During that year, Robert S. Bradley, Peter's tough-minded younger brother, became chairman of AACCo's board of directors and the company's new leader. It was during Robert Bradley's reign that AACCo divested, first its railroad, and then its real estate holdings. Early in 1925, Seaboard Airline Railroad Co. arranged with AACCo to lease CH&N. Three years later, Seaboard acquired all of CH&N's capital stock and absorbed its operations. (In 1958, when the Boca Grande Causeway was completed, Seaboard—by this time its name had been changed to Seaboard Coastline Railroad Company—discontinued passenger service to Boca Grande.)

In June 1925, Joseph P. Day, a New York real estate operator and auctioneer, was retained by the Boca Grande Corporation (the Land Company's new name) to sell the remaining real estate on the island at auction. This decision came about partly because of the Boca Grande Corporation's inability to find purchasers for its land and also because AACCo's directors felt that a fertilizer company should not be in the real estate business. Because of its clear threat to the established character of the island, the proposed auction, which was to be held at the Tampa Bay Hotel on January 29 and 30, 1926, created great anxiety among Boca Grande's residents and greatly upset the beachfront owners and hotel guests. As it turned out, there was no need to be upset; the auction, although heavily promoted, failed to generate any interest in purchasing the rest of the island. AACCo had to continue to try to sell its real estate piecemeal.

In the spring of 1926, Joseph Spadaro, a successful New York contractor, purchased the military reserve from the U.S. government and, in 1929, opened his elegant Boca Grande Hotel south of First Street and east of Gulf Boulevard. The hotel was a large, three-story brick building that consisted of four wings projecting at right angles from a central core. The lavishly appointed lobby was situated in the central area and opened skyward to an eight-sided pyramidal roof constructed at the fourth-floor level. In its early years, the Boca Grande Hotel attracted a glamorous international clientele but, after Spadero's death in 1952, the hotel experienced increasing difficulty in maintaining occupancy and several of its wings had to be closed. In 1961, Bayard and Hugh Sharp and their wives purchased the hotel and its surrounding land. In 1972, the building was, with the help of a deliberately set fire, demolished.

Because of Spadaro's 1926 purchase of the military reserve, the Gasparilla Inn lost its lease on the nine-hole golf course it had been operating at the north end of the reserve for more than a decade. Thus, the Inn found itself without a golf course of its own; moreover, the AACCo directors were not disposed to appropriate funds to build a new one. The thorny problem of obtaining another golf course was finally solved in March 1930, when the Inn was sold to Barron Collier of New York City and Useppa Island who committed himself to build a new 18-hole golf course east of the Inn.

During the ensuing years, the resident superintendent of the Boca Grande Corporation, John E. Riley, continued to sell parcels of land. Finally, the remaining land and lots were sold in December 1945 to Henry L. Schwartz (Sunset Realty Inc.), a wealthy New York oil distributor. By the end of 1945, AACCo's financial involvement in the island had terminated.

In 1897, Albert W. Gilchrist, originally trained as a civil engineer, platted and named the town of Boca Grande. Gilchrist was later elected to two terms in the Florida legislature and then went on to become the 20th governor of the state, serving from 1909 to 1913. (Courtesy of the Florida State Archives.)

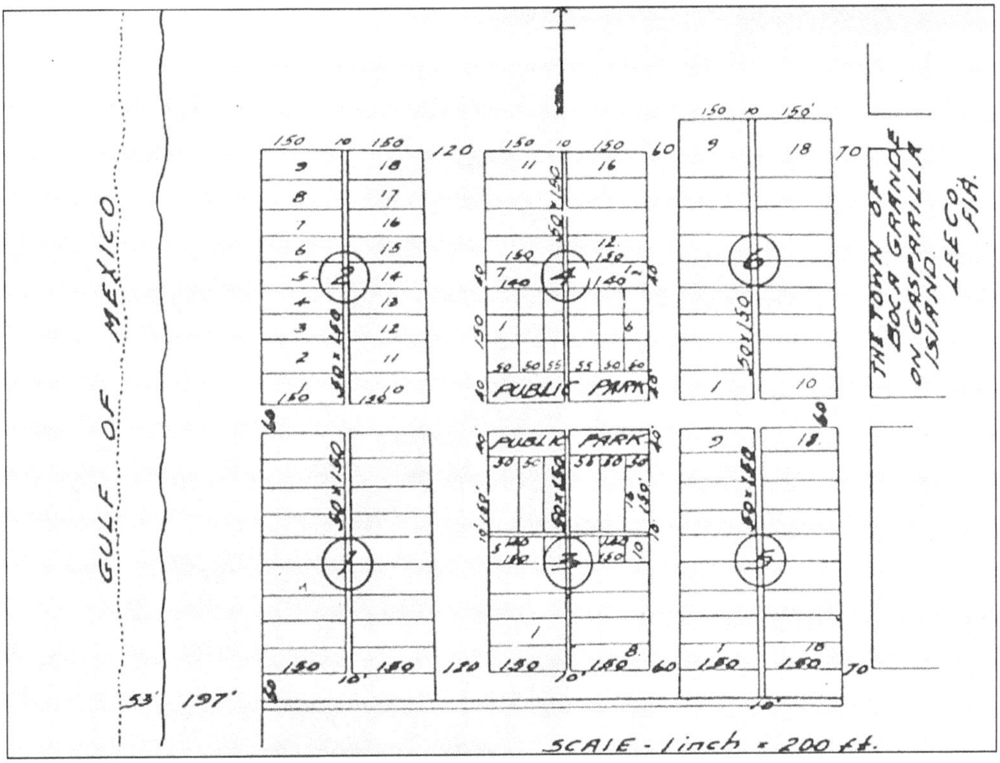

The 1897 Gilchrist plat shows the "Town of Boca Grande on Gasparilla Island, Lee County, FL." It shows the six-block area of what is today First to Third Streets and Gilchrist Avenue to Palm Avenue. (Courtesy of Michael Ingram.)

Peter Butler Bradley (1850–1933) was the oldest son of William Lambert Bradley, a fertilizer magnate of North Weymouth, Massachusetts. In 1899, the Bradleys organized America's first fertilizer conglomerate, the American Agricultural Chemical Company, with Peter becoming its president in 1906. As AACCo's leader for 15 years, Bradley was responsible for the development of Boca Grande, including the creation of the phosphate port at the island's south end and the construction of the Charlotte Harbor and Northern railway, which transported phosphate ore from mines in the Peace River Valley to Port Boca Grande. (Courtesy of the *National Cyclopeadia of American Biography*, 1936.)

Robert S. Bradley, Peter's brother, became chairman of AACCo in 1921. (Courtesy of the Bradley Family Archives.)

Mr. R. S. Bradley

Compliments of
CHARLOTTE HARBOR & NORTHERN RAILWAY COMPANY

James M. Gifford,
PRESIDENT

This Charlotte Harbor and Northern railway pass was issued to Robert S. Bradley in 1915. (Courtesy of the Bradley Family Archives.)

1915 — CHARLOTTE HARBOR & NORTHERN RAILWAY COMPANY — Nº 4

"BOCA GRANDE ROUTE"

PASS Mr. Robert S. Bradley,
ACCOUNT Director, C. H. & N. Ry.

OVER ENTIRE LINE
UNTIL DECEMBER 31st, 1915 — UNLESS OTHERWISE ORDERED AND SUBJECT TO CONDITIONS ON BACK

James M Gifford
PRESIDENT.

A CH&N train is seen here at Boca Grande's first railroad depot, built c. 1907 on Fourth Street in the village. Railroad staff and workmen lived near it. (Courtesy of Florida State Archives.)

As the town of Boca Grande and the phosphate dock at the south end grew, rail traffic increased apace. Shown here is the new and larger brick depot that, in 1911, replaced the earlier wooden one. The view is to the south. Note the water tower, essential to the steam locomotives used at the time. (Courtesy of the Boca Grande Historical Society.)

To accommodate burgeoning railway traffic and the need for more administrative offices for railroad and phosphate operations, the depot was substantially enlarged in 1913. (Courtesy of Florida State Archives.)

The arrival and departure of the train every day was a highlight of village life. Townsfolk gathered at the depot when the train pulled in to see who was arriving and who was departing. The train had both passenger and freight cars, and made three stops on the island: the fishing village of Gasparilla at the north end, downtown Boca Grande, and the phosphate port at the south end. It stopped at the depot in Boca Grande going to and from the port, at about noon and 4 p.m., photo c. 1926 (Courtesy of Pansy Polk Cost.)

A Charlotte Harbor and Northern Railway timetable for February 24, 1924, shows stops from Jacksonville to South Boca Grande. (Courtesy of the Boca Grande Historical Society.)

Visitors to Boca Grande arrive at the depot in the 1940s. Manzy, a popular and well-known porter, is visible under the Western Union sign. Immediately to the right of Manzy is John Crandall, manager of the Boca Grande Hotel, who is welcoming a female guest. (Courtesy of Pansy Polk Cost and Charlyn Crandall Heidenreich.)

Early in 1911, a two-story, red-brick bank opened in Boca Grande on the southeast corner of Fourth Street and East Railroad Avenue. The first floor was occupied by "L.M. Fouts & Sons Bankers." In the 1930s, it operated as the "Florida Bank of Boca Grande," later housing apartments and the United Telephone Station. It was demolished in the early 1980s. Today, the Sprint Telephone building occupies the site. (Courtesy of the *Boca Beacon*.)

The Boca Grande Mercantile Company, established in about 1912, was housed in this building, which is now Boca Grande's post office. Groceries, meats, dry goods, hardware, and furniture were sold here. A fire destroyed most of the Mercantile around 1915, and it was rebuilt as a one-story building. (Courtesy of the *Boca Beacon*.)

In this c. 1912 Fourth Street view, looking east, the depot is to the left and beyond it is Jerome Fugate's two-story drug store, partly blocked by a freight car. Beyond the Mercantile (on the right) are the railroad's water tower and the bank building, which also housed the telephone exchange on its second floor. (Courtesy of the Charlotte Harbor Area Historical Society.)

This is the residence of L.M. Fouts at Gilchrist Avenue and Fourth Street. Fouts was second vice president of the Charlotte Harbor and Northern Railway and was one of the first, if not the first, CH&N official to build a home in Boca Grande. He was also appointed general manager of the Boca Grande Land Company, which was responsible for the construction of the Hotel Boca Grande (to be renamed the Gasparilla Inn). Fouts originally managed the Peace River Phosphate Mining Company for AACCo. In 1905, he was put in charge of the group of workers who landed on Boca Grande to begin construction of the railroad. (Courtesy of Florida State Archives.)

Construction of the Gasparilla Inn—at first called the Hotel Boca Grande—began in 1910, with completion in 1911. Originally, it was designed to house visiting directors and company officers. In its very first season, the 20-room hotel was oversubscribed. By the following year, it had been doubled in size. Based on its success in attracting guests, Peter and Robert Bradley and a senior associate of the company, James M. Gifford, soon decided that the Inn had the potential to become a splendid resort and, in 1913, they hired Karl Abbott, an ambitious young hotel manager, to enlarge and refurbish it further. (Courtesy of Florida State Archives.)

A view of the Gasparilla Inn, seen from Fifth Street looking northwest, shows the structure after its 1914 enlargement. The two pedestrians at the right are dressed for chilly weather. (Courtesy of Florida State Archives.)

The Quick Hotel on Palm Avenue was one of several small inns built to accommodate a growing influx of visitors to Boca Grande. On the left is the Kuhl house, c. 1920. (Courtesy of Jeff Gaines.)

The old post office on Fourth Street is seen here after a rainstorm, c. 1925. (Courtesy of Jeff Gaines.)

The front of this 1926 sales brochure advertises the town of Boca Grande for sale, including "Hotels, Residences and about 1,000 Building Plots." The booklet states inside: "The Seaboard Air Line [R.R.] has recently acquired the owning company's railroad, and in accordance with their policy, the owners are now arranging to dispose of their other properties not required for manufacturing purposes." It goes on to state that the town is "one of the most beautiful and valuable properties in Florida—fully established, permanent, and above all, rich in quick Profit-Making possibilities." (Courtesy of the Boca Grande Historical Society.)

Barron G. Collier purchased the Gasparilla Inn for $150,000 in 1930. This view of the Inn shows its front entrance, to which Collier had added a neoclassical loggia adorned with ten Ionic columns. Collier also created a new 18-hole golf course, most of which was built on a mangrove-covered island to the east of the Inn. (Courtesy of the Gasparilla Inn.)

Mr. and Mrs. Barron G. Collier were possibly standing at the rail of the Collier yacht in this photograph. Collier was an advertising magnate and South Florida real estate developer with homes in New York City and Useppa Island. The Collier family owned the Gasparilla Inn from 1930 until 1963, when it was purchased by a syndicate led by Bayard Sharp. (Courtesy of the Boca Grande Historical Society.)

Many of the guests who stayed at the Gasparilla Inn were ardent fishermen. They formed a sort of fishing club that used the Inn's Pelican Room as its headquarters. Here, fishing yarns were exchanged and some of the more notable trophies were exhibited. This scene probably dates to the 1940s. (Courtesy of the Charlotte Harbor Area Historical Society.)

An aerial view, looking to the east, shows the Gasparilla Inn and its outbuildings in 1925. On the other side of Fifth Street (at left) is the Inn's "casino," which fronts on Palm Avenue. Behind the casino is a tennis court. At the top is the mangrove-covered island that became the Gasparilla Inn's golf course in the 1980s. (Courtesy of the Boca Grande Historical Society.)

The Gasparilla Inn's "bathhouse," or beach club, on the beach at the west end of Fifth Street, seen here about 1910, was destroyed by the hurricane of 1921. (Courtesy of the Charlotte Harbor Area Historical Society.)

Clara Tillis Gaines poses on the steps of the Gasparilla Inn's second bathhouse, c. 1924. (Courtesy of Jeff Gaines.)

Between 1911 and 1914, the grounds of the Gasparilla Inn were landscaped, and the major streets of Boca Grande were lined with trees and shrubs. In this c. 1940 postcard, Fifth Street, looking west, is lined with Australian pines. The trees were uprooted by a hurricane in 1944. (Courtesy of the *Boca Beacon*.)

The Gasparilla Inn casino is seen here from the tennis court. The clothes appear to be of World War I vintage. Far from being a "gambling den," the casino was used for dances, recitals, and other genteel entertainments. (Courtesy of the *Boca Beacon*.)

This is a page from a 1920s CH&N Railway sales brochure. The railroad used every means at its disposal to lure people to Boca Grande, and the strategy worked. The Gasparilla Inn was popular almost overnight with Northerners from cities such as Boston and Philadelphia who had the means to escape the winter. The Inn's first manager, Karl Abbott, wrote, "The Inn caught on in Boston. It was whispered up and down State Street that someone had discovered a little hotel on an island off the Florida coast that catered only to the 'right people.'" (Courtesy of the Boca Grande Historical Society.)

In this c. 1925 aerial view of the town of Boca Grande looking north, the railroad depot and water tower are at center left. The town's few buildings are scattered around the depot with the Gasparilla Inn visible at the upper right. The white building at the lower right is the town's ice storage plant. (Courtesy of the Boca Grande Historical Society.)

Clara Gaines, Mrs. Victor L. Tillis, and Mrs. William T. Speer are pictured in front of the Gasparilla Inn's bandstand in 1929. (Courtesy of Florida State Archives.)

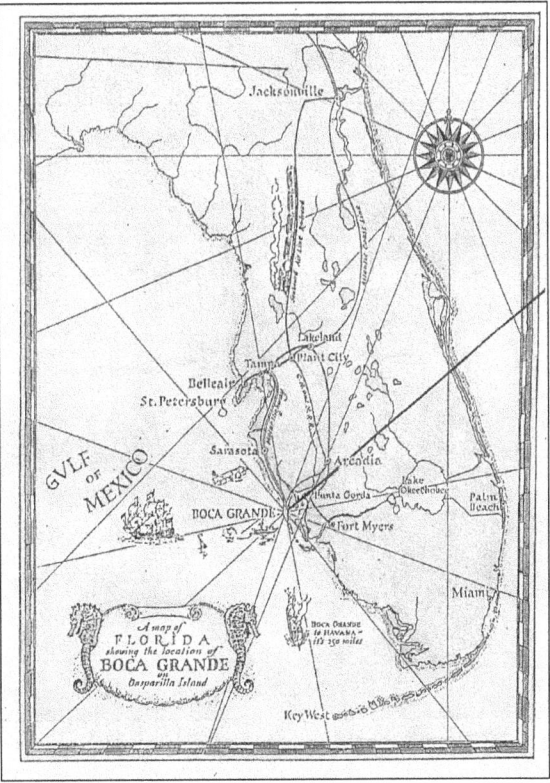

Publications such as this map from a 1930s brochure promoted Boca Grande's charms. This one called Boca Grande "an island colony of quaintly old distinction," stating that "the keynote is simplicity, coupled with a complete outlet for individuality . . . with none of the usual popular appeal . . . no commercialized amusement, no noise, crowds, traffic, conventions, nor real estate developments." (Courtesy of the Boca Grande Lighthouse Museum.)

The Little Inn on Fourth Street was a satellite of the Gasparilla Inn. It was used for summer visitors to the island, when the main Inn was closed for the season. (Courtesy of the Gasparilla Inn.)

The Little Inn burned to the ground in 1943. This photograph shows the burned-out wreckage. (Courtesy of the Boca Grande Historical Society.)

In 1929, Joseph Spadaro opened his elegant Boca Grande Hotel just south of First Street, fronting on Gulf Boulevard. It boasted a golf course, riding stable, landing strip, tennis courts, and a wide stretch of beach on the Gulf of Mexico, and it welcomed many celebrities of the day. (Courtesy Charlyn Crandall Heidenreich.)

The Boca Grande Hotel was a large, solidly constructed three-story brick building that consisted of four wings projecting at right angles from a central core. This aerial view, looking east, shows the hotel with First Street at left. (Courtesy Charlyn Crandall Heidenreich.)

Lighthouse keeper Osmund McKinney, his wife, Lois, and their two small children are pictured in front of the Boca Grande Hotel in 1938. (Courtesy of Evelyn McKinney Ferguson.)

The Boca Grande Hotel had an elegantly appointed dining room, seen here in the 1940s. In promotional literature, Joe Spadaro called the Boca Grande Hotel "the finest hotel on the west coast of Florida." (Courtesy of Evelyn McKinney Ferguson.)

The lavishly appointed and spacious lobby of the Boca Grande Hotel was situated in the central area, opening skyward to an octagonal roof constructed at the fourth-floor level. (Courtesy of the Charlotte Harbor Area Historical Society.)

This c. 1940 postcard provides an idealized picture of the Boca Grande Hotel and its beach. (Courtesy of the *Boca Beacon*.)

This postcard shows the octagonal atrium of the Boca Grande Hotel with its three tiers of balconies. (Courtesy of Pansy Polk Cost.)

Here is the beachhouse of the Boca Grande Hotel in 1952. Note the octagonal roof of the hotel's central atrium that is visible at far left. (Courtesy of Marge Dennis.)

Pictured in the 1940s, from left to right, are John Crandall, manager of the Boca Grande Hotel; Joseph Spadaro, hotel owner; General Kincaid, president of the American Hotel Corporation; and a Mr. George Warton. (Courtesy of Charlyn Crandall Heidenreich.)

The Boca Grande Hotel was demolished by fire and the wrecking ball in 1972. (Courtesy of Marguerite East.)

In 1911 Lee County purchased a lot on Gilchrist Avenue near First Street from the Boca Grande Land Company on which they constructed Boca Grande's first school, a two-story frame building with four classrooms. (Courtesy of the Boca Grande Historical Society.)

As the island's population grew, a new school became necessary. In 1927, winter resident Louise duPont Crowninshield negotiated a land trade with Lee County that allowed the board of education to build a "Mediterranean-style" school building for grades one through twelve at the corner of Park Avenue and First Street. This 1929 photo shows the new school under construction. The building is today the Boca Grande Community Center. (Courtesy of Pansy Polk Cost.)

The new school is shown here after completion in 1929. The cost of the building, $33,492, was paid by the citizens of the town. Students were bused from various parts of the island, and after 1949, a "school boat" brought children from neighboring islands. (Courtesy of the Florida State Archives.)

Located at the eastern end of Banyan (Second) Street, the Boca Grande Community House was built in the late 1930s through the generosity of island resident and benefactor Louise duPont Crowninshield. It was the place for dances, plays, wedding receptions, baby showers, lectures, town meetings, garden shows, bingo parties, fish fries, community Christmas parties, and Kiwanis and Woman's Club meetings. The House—renamed the Louise Crowninshield Community House in 1998—continues to serve Boca Grande as a community meeting place today. (Courtesy of the Boca Grande Lighthouse Museum.)

This is the Boca Grande School graduating class of 1935. (Courtesy of Jeff Gaines.)

Fugate's Department Store is shown here after it moved in 1937 to the west side of the railroad tracks, c. 1940. (Courtesy of the *Boca Beacon*.)

One of Boca Grande's first fire trucks is parked near what appears to be Boca Grande Bayou. (Courtesy of the Boca Grande Fire Department.)

The Gasparilla Inn held a "Bundles for Britain" luncheon at its beach club on February 22, 1941. (Courtesy of the Gasparilla Inn.)

In this Fourth Street view, looking west, note the train in the background. (Courtesy of Jeff Gaines.)

The Johann Fust Community Library, seen here in the 1950s, was built, stocked with books, and donated to the citizens of Boca Grande in 1950 by Roger Amory of Boston and Boca Grande. Amory named it after the man who financed Johannes Gutenberg's 15th-century invention of moveable type, which made mass publishing possible. The beautifully designed building, complete with a landscaped courtyard, has coquina rock walls, a cypress ceiling, and a red tile floor. (Courtesy of the Florida State Archives.)

The Community Library's donor, Roger Amory, was a bibliophile and a collector of rare books. He conceived of the library as not only a place for research, reading, and study, but for quiet contemplation and enjoyment. (Courtesy of the *Boca Beacon*.)

Mrs. Roger Amory aboard the *Papyrus*, the library's "book boat," which brought reading material to folks on Gasparilla's neighboring islands. (Courtesy of the *Boca Beacon*.)

Philanthropist Louise duPont Crowninshield was a winter resident of Boca Grande from about 1917 to 1958. She founded the Boca Grande Health Clinic in 1946. She also founded the Boca Grande Community House, helped start the San Marco Theater, was instrumental in the building of the Boca Grande School, and sponsored the island's Boy Scout troop and field trips for school children. She was sometimes called Boca Grande's "fairy godmother" because of her many generous contributions to the island she loved. (Courtesy of the *Boca Beacon*.)

Louise duPont Crowninshield is pictured here as a young woman. (Courtesy of the *Boca Beacon*.)

This home of the Boca Grande Health Clinic from 1963 until 1990 cost $50,000 to build, and was paid for by island residents. A modern clinic was built and opened in 1990 across the street from the old building which, today, houses the island's police and emergency medical services station. (Courtesy of the *Boca Beacon*.)

Apart from Boca Grande's two major hotels, smaller inns and hostelries also graced the town. These included the Little Inn (a satellite of the Gasparilla Inn), the Sprott Hotel, Mrs. Halloway's Boarding House, the Quick Hotel, the Hotel Palm, and the Palmetto Inn, pictured here in the mid-1950s. (Courtesy of the *Boca Beacon*.)

The San Marco Theatre was built in 1928 by Louise duPont Crowninshield, Henry duPont, Rodney Sharp, and J.E. Riley. In 1948, Roger Amory purchased and restored the theater, which had been damaged in the 1944 hurricane. Three nights a week during the winter, and once a week in summer, the theater played the latest Hollywood movies to a full house. It had a shell floor, a tin roof, box seats, and a balcony reserved for the island's African-American residents. The theater closed in 1977. (Painting by Jack Barndollar; from *A Very Special Island* by Betty Barndollar.)

The abandoned theater, pictured here in the late 1970s, was later purchased and transformed into a restaurant and shops. (Courtesy of the *Boca Beacon*.)

Ice was delivered to island residences and businesses on this ice wagon during the early days. (Courtesy of Jeff Gaines.)

Murdock was a town character and is seen here with his pet monkey. He used to make "skeeter beaters" out of palm fronds and sell them at the movie theater. (Courtesy of the *Boca Beacon*.)

Boca Grande has always been a boater's paradise and has several marinas today. The oldest is Whidden's Marina, shown here in 1930, four years after it was built. In the early days, it was also a night spot, dance hall, and restaurant. (Courtesy of the *Boca Beacon*.)

Miller's Marina, sponsor of the famous "Tarpon Tide" Tarpon Tournaments, is the second-oldest marina on the island. It was built in 1952 and is featured on this *c.* 1960 postcard. (Courtesy of the *Boca Beacon*.)

The First Baptist Church of Boca Grande was organized in 1910, and services were initially held in the town's first school building. The present building, shown here, was built in 1915. (Courtesy of the *Boca Beacon*.)

St. Andrew's Episcopal Church was originally a wooden cottage that was moved to its present location on Gilchrist Avenue and converted to a church in about 1912. (Courtesy of the *Boca Beacon*.)

Our Lady of Mercy Mission was designed in Italian Renaissance style by F. Burrall Hoffman in 1949 and completed in 1950. Its elegant entry's wooden doors were taken from an old Spanish monastery. Hoffman, a nationally known architect who in earlier years had designed several vacation houses in Boca Grande, was 67 years old when he drew up the plans for this lovely Roman Catholic chapel, his final architectural gift to Boca Grande. (Courtesy of the Boca Grande Lighthouse Museum.)

The United Methodist Church, situated on the northeast corner of Gilchrist Avenue and Fourth Street, was constructed in 1910. (Courtesy of the *Boca Beacon*.)

Banyan Street, one of Boca Grande's most noted landmarks, was planted in about 1916. It is shown here in about 1950. (Courtesy of Jeff Gaines.)

Fishing nets dry on a large net wheel on Boca Grande Bayou, c. 1950. (Courtesy of the *Boca Beacon* and Dr. Dennis Dorsey.)

Henry L. Schwartz purchased most of the north end of the island in 1945. (Courtesy of the *Boca Beacon*.)

The abandoned and forlorn-looking railroad depot is pictured here before its purchase and restoration by Ramar Group Companies beginning in 1978. Today it is on the National Register of Historic Places and houses a restaurant, shops, and offices. (Courtesy of the *Boca Beacon*.)

Five

GETTING THERE: TRANSPORTATION ON A BARRIER ISLAND

Stores, businesses, boardinghouses, and residences began to spring up in the new village of Boca Grande almost as soon as the Gasparilla Inn opened for business in 1911. Sunday excursions by train brought increasing numbers of people who came to the island for its unmatched beaches on the sparkling Gulf of Mexico. Some saw opportunities on the island, and bought property and built homes. A growing village meant growing employment opportunities. New people came to town, new businesses sprang up, a new bridge was built across Boca Grande Bayou (which had been dredged to accommodate good-sized boats), and better facilities for boats were built, at East Dock and later, the "L-dock."

Boca Grande's growing population encompassed a great variety of people. Lighthouse keepers, pilots, port employees, railroad personnel, merchants and commercial fishermen crossed paths daily with hotel employees, a variety of laborers, sailors from all over the world, tarpon fishing guides, bankers, anglers arriving to fish for tarpon, and wealthy winter residents. By 1920, Boca Grande had become a flourishing, unique, and dynamic island community.

The railroad was of course the catalyst for all this development, and it was the only way, other than by private boat, that one could reach Boca Grande in the early years. Travelers could board Seaboard Air Line's Silver Star in New York, have Pullman cars and a diner at their disposal, and arrive in Boca Grande 24 to 26 hours later.

Getting quality medical care on an isolated barrier island was a challenge in the early years. Except for the quarantine doctor at the port, Boca Grande had no doctor. During the winter season, a physician was brought in for guests of the Gasparilla Inn, and he sometimes treated other patients. The port's quarantine doctor sometimes saw patients as well. If an illness or injury was serious, islanders had to travel to Tampa or Arcadia by train. In case of emergency, a patient was loaded onto a special flatbed rail "ambulance" pulled by an electric rail car for transport across the railroad trestle to the mainland.

The first owner of an automobile on Gasparilla Island, according to Capt. Carey Johnson in his memoirs, was Capt. Kingsmore Johnson Sr., who purchased a new Model T Ford in Punta Gorda and brought it to the island on the Chadwick Brothers' fish "run boat," the *Iris*. It was unloaded on East Dock at the foot of Fourth Street. The one-way cost for this service was $25. By the early 1920s, there were some 15 or 20 cars on the island.

The stage was set, by the late 1920s, for some entrepreneur to offer residents and visitors a form of alternative transportation to and from the island, and that is just what Capt. William C. Sprott did. It was about the mid-1920s when Captain Sprott took over operation of the Palmetto Inn on Palm Avenue. He decided that there must be a way to get both guests and their vehicles over to Boca Grande from the mainland. He owned a small cabin cruiser, the *Beth*, so he acquired a barge large enough to carry one automobile and, through some persistence, obtained a landing site on the east side of the island about a mile north of the village and another site across Gasparilla Sound at Placida. Thus, in 1927, the Boca Grande Ferry Company was born.

That first year saw the installation of a larger barge capable of carrying two cars. When an even larger barge was purchased, Capt. John Riggs, a fine boat builder, was hired to rebuild it into the ferry boat *Catherine*, named for the youngest of Captain Sprott's seven daughters. Originally powered by gasoline, the self-propelled, 64-foot ferry was repowered with a diesel engine. She made the trip to Placida, loaded with nine cars, in about 45 minutes.

It was only a few years until the *Catherine*, making four round trips a day, was unable to handle all the traffic, and Captain Sprott, now assisted by his son Gene, sought again to upgrade his service by looking for a bigger ferry. He found it in 1946 in Saugerties, New York, just south of Albany. Captains Gene Sprott, Roy Pouncey, and Brad Bylaska traveled to New York, where they boarded the *Saugerties*, as the ferry was called, and brought it to Boca Grande via the Hudson River, the East Coast, and across Florida on the Okeechobee Waterway.

Capt. Sprott ran the Boca Grande ferry service until 1952, when he sold it. The new owner ran the service until 1958, when the Boca Grande Bridge and Causeway opened and ferries were no longer needed.

Boca Grande had a streetcar from 1910 to 1920. It was an elaborate electric-powered car owned by the Charlotte Harbor and Northern Railroad and it ran on the railroad tracks between Boca Grande and South Dock (Port Boca Grande). It accommodated about 30 passengers and was powered by large storage batteries, which were recharged at the south end powerhouse every night. (Courtesy of the Boca Grande Historical Society.)

Workers, tourists, commuters—anyone who needed a lift between Boca Grande and South Dock—all used the streetcar, seen here at the downtown railroad depot, c. 1915. (Courtesy of the Charlotte Harbor Area Historical Society.)

Island residents take a ride in a Model-T Ford. The driver is believed to be Troy Speer. (Courtesy of the Charlotte Harbor Area Historical Society.)

Occasionally, cars were brought over to the island by rail. Seen here are the Savarese children sitting in a motorized section car, nicknamed "The Bull," towing their father's DeSoto on a flatbed rail car from Placida to Boca Grande. (Courtesy of Suzanne Harris Savarese and Joseph A. Savarese Jr.)

These people are shown driving onto the ferry in the late 1920s. (Courtesy of Jeff Gaines.)

Gasparilla Island's isolation is clear in this 1925 aerial photograph. With the exception of Gasparilla village, the northern portion of the island is a wilderness. The railroad trestle and tracks going down the island are clearly visible. (Courtesy of the Boca Grande Historical Society.)

The *Saugerties*, pictured here about 1948, carried up to 11 vehicles and made five round trips a day to Placida. (Courtesy of Jeff Gaines.)

The *Catherine* (right) is docked at the ferry landing while the *Saugerties* loads cars, about 1950. The cost was $5 per car for "locals," $8 for visitors, and the trip took about 45 minutes. The *Catherine* was laid up in the early 1950s; the sturdy old *Saugerties* continued in service until the causeway came in 1958. (Courtesy of the Boca Grande Historical Society.)

If you needed to get to or from the mainland in a hurry, but without a vehicle, you could hire Bert Cole, who owned a garage in Placida and ran a water taxi service. Note the tall gravity fed gas pump behind the boat. (Courtesy of the *Boca Beacon*.)

The *Saugerties*n is shown here on the way to Gasparilla Island from Placida in the 1950s. (Courtesy of the *Boca Beacon*.)

The abandoned ferry landing at Loomis Flats on Gasparilla Island is pictured here, c. 1960. Near the site today, a plaque marks the existence of the once indispensable Boca Grande Ferry Service. (Courtesy of the *Boca Beacon*.)

The 1.7-mile-long Boca Grande Causeway and its swing bridge for boats traveling the Intracoastal Waterway was built in 1957–1958 by the Florida Bridge Company of St. Petersburg. The causeway connects the mainland near Placida (upper left) to the north end of Gasparilla Island (lower right). Running parallel to the causeway, the old railroad trestle crossing Gasparilla Sound is visible. In 1983, the Florida Bridge Company sold the causeway to Gaspar Associates of Pinellas County. In May 1996, the Florida legislature established a unit of local government called the Gasparilla Island Bridge Authority to own, operate, and maintain the causeway and bridge on behalf of the public. In January 1998, Gaspar Associates sold the causeway to the Bridge Authority for $7.9 million. (Courtesy of Dusty Hopkins.)

Passenger train service to Boca Grande ended shortly after the causeway was built in 1958, but the phosphate trains continued to roll up and down the island. The last train to leave Boca Grande in 1981 was pulled by Seaboard Engine No. 344. (Courtesy of Kay and Charles Dana Gibson.)

Just about the entire population of the island showed up to watch and photograph the last train leave the island in 1981. (Courtesy of Kay and Charles Dana Gibson.)

The last train heads east on the railroad trestle across Gasparilla Sound. The metal swing bridge was purchased and ended up in New York State in the mid-1980s. (Courtesy of Kay and Charles Dana Gibson.)

Six

HURRICANES

Boca Grande's first experience with a hurricane in the 20th century occurred in 1910. Anthony B. Arnold, in his unpublished monograph on Boca Grande's early history, states that "in October 1910, a hurricane accompanied by heavy rain washed out two or three miles of soft, freshly made CH & N railroad embankment along the upper Peace River." The late Thomas Parkinson, who lived in Boca Grande for more than 60 years, remembered that, during the 1910 hurricane, several fishermen's stilt homes on Punta Blanco (near Cayo Costa) were washed away, and that two men crossed the bay on the roof of one of them.

Author C.D. Gibson also refers to the destructive power of this hurricane: "As the 1910 hurricane approached Charlotte Harbor, a number of Cuban fishing vessels took shelter on the harbor side of Cayo Costa. Realizing that they would soon be on a lee shore if they stayed at Cayo Costa, the Cuban skippers decided to run up under the protection of Bokeelia . . . By the time the wind (which was backing into the east) reached its maximum velocity, the smacks [sailboats] were fully exposed to the brunt of steep seas building up over the width of Charlotte Harbor. Anchored as they were in shallow water, their keels began to pound harder and harder against the bottom and one by one, the smacks broke up and their entire crews (except for one boy) were drowned. Since that day, the cove near 'Tariva's Bayou' [named for Tariva Padilla] where many of the bodies washed ashore, has been referred to as Dead Man's Cove."

Longtime residents of Boca Grande retain vivid memories of hurricanes and severe tropical storms that have lashed the island over the years. However, recollections of the dates of these events have sometimes been in conflict. For example, old time residents of Boca Grande remember that there was a severe hurricane in 1921 that produced widespread flooding and, among other injuries, destroyed the Gasparilla Inn's bathhouse on the Gulf at the foot of Fifth Street. However, photographs in the Florida Archives (donated by the Speer family), which show destruction of "a" bathhouse and of areas of Gasparilla Island submerged under several feet of water, are dated 1926.

An examination of the U.S. Weather Bureau's hurricane records for 1926 shows that a deadly hurricane did indeed pass directly over Charlotte Harbor on September 21, 1926, heading northwest. In 1921, however, only one hurricane hit Florida, and the Weather Bureau records show it crossing the peninsula from west to east to the north of Tampa. Nevertheless, it appears that, before it came ashore, the 1921 hurricane hovered for two days in the Gulf just to the west of Boca Grande. During that time, the high waters and strong winds generated by the storm were extremely destructive to Gasparilla Island (based on local anecdotal evidence), and it is the authors' belief that it was indeed the 1921 hurricane that destroyed the Gasparilla Inn's first bathhouse on the Gulf. (Regarding the 1926 date on the photographs in the Florida Archives, it is plausible that after the first bathhouse was destroyed in 1921, the Inn would have rebuilt it; that bathhouse, in its turn, might well have been demolished in 1926. It is not possible to determine this with certainty; unfortunately, most of the Gasparilla Inn's records of the period were destroyed when the Little Inn burned in 1943.)

There is considerable oral history regarding the 1921 hurricane and its local effects. Anson Gaskill, son of fishing guide Harry Gaskill, had good reason to remember this storm and his memories of it are recorded by authors Lindsey Williams and U.S. Cleveland: "Daddy stayed at a camp near Boca Grande Pass. On weekends, when fishing was suspended, he would row over to the quarantine station at Cayo Costa, or the lighthouse on Gasparilla Island for company . . . I was born May 21, 1912 . . . We had a terrible hurricane in 1921. It blew into the harbor, raising the highest tide I have ever seen. Daddy woke us at 3 a.m. and said we had to leave because the water was coming into the house. We started for the school which was made of brick and had a second floor. I waded in water up to my waist . . . We had to stay there that night, the next day, and the next night before the water went down enough for us to come home."

Fisherman Albert Lowe, who was living at Gasparilla (village) at the north end of the island in 1921, said (in a late 1980s interview with the *Boca Beacon*) that nearly all the homes on Cole Island were washed away in the 1921 hurricane. Clara Futch, another Gasparilla resident, said there were fishing boats tied up to her front porch, and Tommy Parkinson said the 1921 storm brought water as high as it has ever been on Gasparilla Island. Another resident, Homer Addison, remembered that it was the 1921 storm that washed away the Gasparilla Inn's beach ("bath") house on the Gulf. Sam Black, a railroad employee, told his brother-in-law Jefferson Gaines Jr. this tale about the 1921 hurricane: "It came out of the south. The wind had been higher in other storms, but this one had the water. The island took a pounding for two days from the waves and high tides. The beach downtown really changed too. The pavilion [bath house] and Gulf Boulevard washed away . . . South of town also got it bad."

Williams and Cleveland (1996) have described what happened during the 1926 hurricane: "The Florida hurricane of 1926 blew the water of Lake Okeechobee against the southwestern dike, breached it, and within 10 minutes flooded the town of Moore Haven to a depth of seven feet. The official report listed 130 residents of Moore Haven drowned, but dozens of others were unaccounted for. Throughout south Florida, 373 persons were killed and 6,281 injured . . . The most curious effect of the hurricane was blowing all water out of upper Charlotte Harbor as the storm approached, then blowing it back to flood Punta Gorda and Charlotte Harbor Town as it passed."

There is wide agreement that the hurricane of 1944 caused extensive damage to Gasparilla Island. The Weather Bureau Hurricane Tracking Chart for that year shows that the one hurricane striking Florida in 1944 was spawned in the Caribbean, crossed over Cuba's western end, and then made landfall in the Charlotte Harbor area. It was in the 1944 hurricane that Boca Grande lost many of its tall trees. Old-timers remember pines crisscrossed everywhere downtown and that a whole mile of railroad track at the "Narrows" north of town was torn up. Tommy Parkinson said that two boxcars were moved about a block by the wind. Another longtime islander, the late Gene Bowe, told the *Boca Beacon* that the winds during this storm were 150 miles an hour. He said that for a week there were no trains, until the tracks were repaired. "All the wires were down. Water came clear across the south end of the island. The wind leveled just about everything," Bowe said. Gibson says that the 1944 storm washed out the county road at the south end, south of the "s" curve.

Apart from occasional hurricanes, Boca Grande has weathered many severe tropical storms during the 20th century. These gales repeatedly damaged seawalls and eroded the beaches. In June 1982, for example, a southerly gale caused flooding in various parts of the island, particularly at the south end. Because of these storms, the road that for many years wound along the Gulf shore at the south end was finally abandoned in 1989.

The bathhouse of the Gasparilla Inn experiences the onslaught of hurricane winds and waves in 1921. (Courtesy of Homer Addison.)

The bathhouse is seen here after the 1921 hurricane. (Courtesy of Homer Addison.)

Flooding occurred around the Gasparilla Inn during the hurricane of 1921. (Courtesy of Homer Addison.)

Flood waters of the 1921 hurricane surround the Gasparilla Inn's bandstand situated on Palm Avenue directly across the street from the Inn's front entrance. (Courtesy of Homer Addison.)

The Little Inn was also surrounded by floodwaters in the 1921 hurricane. (Courtesy of Homer Addison.)

This downtown street, probably Gilchrist Avenue, flooded in the 1921 storm. (Courtesy of Homer Addison.)

Damage to AACCo's phosphate dock was caused by the hurricane of 1921. (Courtesy of Homer Addison.)

An aerial view of the "Narrows" north of the village of Boca Grande in 1925 shows just how vulnerable this thin stretch of island is to storms. A spit of sand is seemingly all that connects the land in this photograph. (Courtesy of the Gasparilla Inn.)

The railroad tracks were totally undermined at the Narrows after the 1944 hurricane. There were no trains for a week, until the tracks were shored up and repaired. (Courtesy of the *Boca Beacon*.)

Port Boca Grande was severely damaged by the 1926 hurricane. (Courtesy of Jeff Gaines.)

This picture provides additional evidence of the destruction to the port that resulted from the 1926 hurricane. (Courtesy of Jeff Gaines.)

Seven

The Beachfront

As soon as the Boca Grande Land Company was chartered to sell real estate by the State of Florida in 1907, its directors, Peter Bradley and James M. Gifford, set about developing Boca Grande as an upscale winter resort. In the words of Anthony B. Arnold, a senior officer of the American Agricultural Chemical Company who worked closely with Bradley, "To assure a high class development, the Land Company restricted the lots on Gulf Boulevard and Gilchrist Avenue to the building of residences only, and at a minimum cost of $4,000 and $3,500 respectively." About 1914, Francis B. Crowninshield, an artist from Marblehead, Massachusetts, and his wife, Louise duPont Crowninshield, built a cottage on Gulf Boulevard at First Street. Soon thereafter, Harry F. duPont, Louise Crowninshield's brother, built a cottage in the same block. Several additional houses were built on Gulf Boulevard by railroad employees. It would be a dozen years before any more lots were sold or houses built along the beach.

In the fall of 1925, Robert Bradley asked Arnold to spend the winter in Boca Grande and prepare for the forthcoming auction of AACCo's remaining real estate, scheduled to take place in Tampa, January 29 and 30, 1926. In the meantime, he was instructed to sell whatever land he could. In the fulfillment of his assignment, Arnold had the effective assistance of Colonel L.J. Campbell, who was staying at the Inn at the time. Campbell was still recovering from having been severely wounded and gassed in World War I. Being the son of the president of the Youngstown Sheet and Tube Company, he was well-connected socially and was able to aid Arnold in his efforts to burnish AACCo's image with finicky Inn guests. He also helped in the search for desirable purchasers of the company's unsold land.

Campbell and his wife, Cordelia, purchased a beachfront house on April 15, 1925. In December, Hugh Rodney Sharp, brother-in-law of Pierre S. duPont, purchased a 575-foot beachfront lot. (The original Sharp house was substantially enlarged and remodeled during the ensuing years.) The sale to Sharp was the first of many consummated that winter. To the great embarrassment of AACCo's management (and the great relief of Boca Grande's winter residents), the January auction was a complete failure, with little or no public interest being shown in the purchase of Boca Grande real estate.

Beach erosion was recognized to be a serious problem by Boca Grande's earliest residents. Gilchrist's 1897 plat showed 197 feet of high ground and 53 feet of beach west of blocks one and two. A survey conducted in 1925 showed only 15 feet of high ground and a very narrow beach. In 1924, C.R. Peterkin, employed by AACCo to promote the sale of the company's real estate holdings, attempted to stem the erosion by placing semicircular rows of palmetto logs along the beach. These feeble barriers were washed away by the first storm. By then, various storms had destroyed Gulf Avenue—the wide street that ran along the shoreline from First Street to north of Thirteenth Street—and the trees that lined it. In a number of places, portions of lots fronting on the beach had begun to show serious erosion. It became evident that some action had to be taken to protect the beachfront property. However, AACCo was not about to pay for the needed repairs. As Arnold put it, "The Company had spent enough money and was in no mood to build a proper retaining wall and jetties to protect a half a mile of beach front. No one owner could protect his alone."

Following this line of thinking, Arnold, in 1925, proposed to the Crowninshields that they buy (from AACCo) the riparian rights to the property in blocks one, two, and three for $1. This action was to be followed by the formation of a group to take responsibility for building suitable retaining walls and jetties and paying the bills. This approach, which set the pattern for future collective anti-erosion measures, proved acceptable to the property owners and, in 1927, a seawall made up of a line of piles backed up by three layers of lapped cypress sheathing was constructed.

By the late 1940s, this wooden structure had begun to deteriorate and a local contractor, S. Findley Griffin, was hired to build a concrete sea wall in front of the properties of the six residents who lived between Seventh and Thirteenth Streets. Late in 1948, the remaining beachfront residents, from First Street north to Seventh Street, decided to repair the wooden bulkhead already in place with treated pile. The cost was estimated to be $35 per foot, compared to nearly $52 per foot for a new concrete sea wall and sidewalk. On June 29, 1949, Griffin was asked to proceed with the installation of the treated pilings.

Peter Ffolliott, a "beachfronter" since 1961, has traced the history of the sea wall from First to Fourth Street. He notes that just two years after its repair in 1949, the wooden seawall had already begun to suffer damage from erosion. In an effort to protect the wall and the beach, the property owners had eight jetties placed at intervals between First and Fourth Streets. They were only partly effective in arresting the erosion. Writes Ffolliott, "Time passed and by 1951 the old neighborhood began to change and so did the wooden sea wall. Each passing year more damage and erosion was evident."

In 1967, a contract with Misener Marine Construction of St. Petersburg was approved by the property owners (who were sometimes referred to as the "seven sons of the beach," although three of the owners were women). The plan called for the construction of a formidable, well-anchored wall of reinforced concrete 8 inches thick. The cost was $63 per front foot.

Although the new concrete wall remained pretty much intact, the beach kept getting smaller and smaller. Eight "dog-bone" jetties placed along the beach in a zigzag fashion did little to preserve the remaining sand. In Ffolliott's words, "In a few short years no sand was left at all on our beaches. So to protect the now bare concrete sea wall from receiving the full brunt of the wave action, the property owners decided that a rock rip-rap revetment should be placed in front of the seawall. [This action was taken in 1973.] Thirteen years later [1986] it didn't look good. Not only had the rocks making up the rip-rap moved and appeared to have melted . . . but now what had been a sturdy cap on the cement sea wall was showing signs of deterioration . . . Hence, in 1987, additional rip-rap was added and a completely new 24-inch, 710-foot-long cement cap replaced the chipped and cracked old one."

It is interesting to recall that until about 1925, a broad boulevard lined with trees separated the beachfront cottages from the Gulf. After 1925, these cottages truly "fronted" on the beach. For their owners, the erosion that destroyed the boulevard was, in a sense, a gift from the sea that afforded them enhanced privacy and added to the value of their property. At the same time, the vulnerability of the protective bulkheads to further erosion was a continuing source of anxiety and expense.

Today, there is little or no beach left along the Gulf shores of downtown Boca Grande. Periodic beach renourishment—using sand from the dredging of the ships' channel into Port Boca Grande—serves to build up the beach for a short time, but generally, within a matter of months, the sand is swept away by the double action of the natural southerly current along the shoreline and the waves crashing against the seawall.

A title document shows the line of successive owners of a beachfront property, beginning with James A. Newsome, who was one of several people granted an official "land patent" prior to the platting of the downtown area by Gilchrist in 1897. (Courtesy of Peter Ffolliott.)

```
                    From
            UNITED STATES OF AMERICA
                     to
        JAMES A. NEWSOME, ON APRIL 16, 1889
                     to
       ALBERT W. GILCHRIST, ON MARCH 31, 1890
                     to
   BOCA GRANDE LAND COMPANY, ON NOVEMBER 1, 1907
                     to
  W. J. and KATHERINE W. GILLIGAN, ON JULY 29, 1910
                     to
   WILLARD W. and ANNA D. CLOCK, ON APRIL 20, 1917
                     to
  L. J. and CORDELIA C. CAMPBELL, ON APRIL 15, 1925
                     to
   EVANDER B. and SOPHIE SCHLEY, ON MARCH 4, 1934
                     to
      ISABELLA TYSON GILPIN, ON JUNE 25, 1947
                     to
         E. G. SCARRITT, ON MAY 24, 1952
                     to
     MARION WEBER SCARRITT, ON JANUARY 26, 1956
                     to
 PHILLIP M. and BETTY V. RASMUSSEN, ON APRIL 17, 1957
                     to
GEORGE J. L. and ELEANOR H. GRISWOLD, ON AUGUST 8, 1961
                     to
     GEORGE and LYNN PALERMO, ON DECEMBER 31, 1986
```

The original Gulf Boulevard, c. 1919, is pictured in this view, looking south toward First Street from a concrete platform built by the Gasparilla Inn at the end of Fifth Street. This wide thoroughfare, constructed in about 1910, ran between the beachfront lots and the Gulf. By 1925, it had been entirely destroyed by beach erosion. (Courtesy of Jeff Gaines.)

Coping was poured to cover the beachfront bulkhead in 1927. (Courtesy of the Charlotte Harbor Area Historical Society.)

The cypress bulkhead and jetty in front of L.J. Campbell's house are pictured in 1927. Note that sand is piled up on the north side of the jetty and lost on its south side. (Courtesy of the Charlotte Harbor Area Historical Society.)

In this 1952 image, the concrete seawall and the old cypress bulkhead meet at the end of Seventh Street. (Courtesy of Marge Dennis.)

Here is a typical beach slope and width along the downtown seawall and revetment in 1978. Today there is even less beach in front of the same seawall. (Courtesy of the Gasparilla Island Conservation and Improvement Association.)

Even seawalls can't protect beachfront property when high waves crash over them. This photo, showing major erosion behind the downtown Boca Grande seawall, was taken in the early 1990s after a tropical storm. (Courtesy of the *Boca Beacon*.)

Eight

Tarpon Fishing

On March 12, 1885, New York sportsman W.H. Wood caught a 93-pound tarpon on rod and reel at the mouth of the Caloosahatchee River to the south of Boca Grande. His feat was given wide publicity, and a new sport, which would have an immense economic impact on Southwest Florida, and on Boca Grande, was born—the sport of tarpon fishing. The tarpon industry today is a multi-million dollar business on Gasparilla Island. Each spring, tens of thousands of these giant fish, called "silver kings" because of their flashing silver scales, migrate like clockwork into Boca Grande Pass and stay for about three months.

The Spanish named the deep water pass separating Gasparilla and Cayo Costa (La Costa) islands "Boca Grande," meaning "large mouth," for it is where the waters of Charlotte Harbor and the Gulf of Mexico flow swiftly with every tide. Scientists believe that tarpon gather in estuarine areas in preparation for their journey to offshore spawning grounds, perhaps coming to Boca Grande Pass to gorge themselves on the abundance of "pass crabs" and other food swept in and out on the tides daily. So many of the fish congregate in Boca Grande Pass from April through July that the pass is known as the "Tarpon Capital of the World."

Within about a year of Wood's famous catch, the railroad to Punta Gorda, on the east side of Charlotte Harbor, was completed, making it possible for wealthy anglers to arrive in the area with relative ease. The pursuit caught the imagination of sporting gentry on both sides of the Atlantic, creating a major boom in tourism. By 1900, tarpon anglers from England and New England were anchoring their steam yachts in the harbor at the south end of Gasparilla Island, near Boca Grande Pass. Whether they came by rail or yacht, they were all seeking one thing—the thrill of hooking into and landing a tarpon, one of the world's greatest gamefish.

In 1894, Chicago streetcar magnate John M. Roach, who was an avid fisherman, purchased tiny Useppa Island, Gasparilla's neighbor to the southeast. In 1898, he built the Useppa Inn, a 40-room, plushly furnished Victorian hotel, to cater to the elite group that came each year to fish for tarpon, as well as for the harbor's other abundant gamefish such as redfish, trout, and pompano. Useppa became an elegant resort, reigning as one of the prime fishing resorts in the world for several decades.

In 1908, Southwest Florida developer Barron Collier purchased Useppa from Roach and began an aggressive marketing campaign to promote Useppa as the center of tarpon fishing in Charlotte Harbor. On nearby Punta Blanca, Collier built a boatyard and 26 homes for workers, as well as a school. Useppa would remain the headquarters of the local industry until slowly superseded by its larger neighbor, Gasparilla Island, which by 1912 had direct rail connections up and down the East Coast. Useppa was then, and remains today, accessible only by boat.

Collier became the "tarpon king" of the world. He bought or created a string of resorts from Tampa to the Everglades, including Useppa and the Gasparilla Inn on Boca Grande, which he purchased in 1930 and that the Collier family owned until 1963. He eventually owned 3 million acres of land in Southwest Florida and was in large part responsible for its development.

The islands of Charlotte Harbor, including Gasparilla and its neighbors Useppa and Cayo Costa, were pioneered by commercial fishermen who worked for the Cuban salt fish industry. It was from the ranks of the descendants of these fishermen—and from the men who later came to work in the harbor's "ice fish" industry—that many of Boca Grande's early tarpon fishing guides came. After 1900, many of these men would fish commercially much of the year and guide anglers to hunt the mighty "silver king" during April, May, and June. Some of their descendants are today members of the Boca Grande Fishing Guides Association.

Fishing for giant tarpon in the early years, from small canoes and rowboats, required courage and skill on the part of both guide and angler. In Boca Grande Pass, fishing was done during slack tides. The guide would maneuver the small wooden boat into the tarpon. When the angler hooked up, the guide did his best to row the boat to the shoreline, where the angler would fight the fish and attempt to land it. The advent of gasoline engines occurred around 1910 and soon the earlier method of fighting tarpon became outmoded.

The early reels, known as "thumb busters" or "knuckle busters," had no adjustable drag, only a piece of leather with which to thumb the spool of line. The reel handles spun wildly as the racing tarpon melted linen line off the spool. In 1902, Edward vom Hofe of New York City and Useppa patented the world's first reel with an automatic drag. By the early 1900s, a special kind of cane bamboo had replaced the old Calcutta cane, hazel, and ash formerly used to make rods. These two inventions revolutionized the tackle industry and gave anglers a better chance of landing a big tarpon.

Early accounts of tarpon fishing, in books, newspaper accounts and promotional literature, served to attract anglers to Boca Grande Pass, and certainly played a role in the development of Boca Grande. They also are indicative of the thrill, still experienced by thousands of anglers who converge on Boca Grande Pass each spring, of hooking into a fish that many say is unparalleled for its fighting spirit. Some excerpts follow:

The line was flying out again as the tarpon plunged into the depths, and regained all I had won. Then ensued a long uphill fight which I can only compare to a hand-to-hand tussle with a wild beast. (Angler Robert Grant, 1898.)

One of the most glorious sights I know is the dashing action of a tarpon when hooked ... he shoots straight out of the water, with rolling eye and shaking with fury. The tarpon then, with mighty power, goes off in one rush, perhaps a hundred yards, without stopping. (Angler Rowland Ward, 1898.)

When struck, your tarpon may leap straight up, or at an angle, or he may skim along the surface of the water . . . He may speed like a race horse away from you until your 600 feet of line runs out, or he may dash straight for your skiff, rubbing against it, diving under it, or even leaping over it and tangling you in your own line. (Angler A.W. Dimock, 1908.)

W.R. Yiser of Cincinnati landed a 95-pound tarpon in five and half seconds today—in his lap. The fish, on its very first wild leap, jumped into Mr. Yiser's lap and refused to evacuate until it had wrecked about $75 worth of fishing tackle and boat equipment. (*Tampa Tribune* article on an incident in Boca Grande Pass, 1935.)

Tarpon fishing has become a cult. One man I know has caught 1,375 tarpon in the last 25 years and hopes to make it 1,400 before his fishing days are over. (Karl L. Bickel, 1942.)

The largest tarpon ever recorded in Boca Grande Pass, caught in 1983, weighed 234 pounds. The Florida record is 243 pounds; the world record is 283 pounds.

To facilitate tarpon anglers who wanted to be as near Boca Grande Pass as they could, Useppa's first owner, John M. Roach, had a big barge outfitted as a "floating hotel" around 1900 and anchored it near Punta Blanca, 2 miles northwest of Useppa Island. Anglers would stay on it, and local fishing guides would pick them up and row them to the pass for a day's fishing. (Courtesy of the Gasparilla Inn.)

In the first few decades of the tarpon fishing industry, many thousands of the fish were caught, killed, and displayed, sometimes by the dozens, for picture taking, as exemplified in this old postcard. By 1920, members of Useppa's private fishing club, the Izaak Walton Club, had pioneered the "catch and release" concept of fishing. It soon became popular not to kill a tarpon unless it was to be mounted, and the numbers of fish killed greatly declined. Today's recreational tarpon fishery is one of the most highly regulated in the world. Nearly all tarpon caught today in Boca Grande Pass are released. (Courtesy of the *Boca Beacon*.)

The president of the Izaak Walton Club, Useppa's private fishing club, poses with a giant tarpon in 1914. (Courtesy of the Gasparilla Inn.)

In this 1905 photograph, wooden rowboats, roped together, are being towed out to Boca Grande Pass by the Useppa steam yacht *Valima*. The anglers rode aboard the yacht, and the guides rode in the rowboats. Once in the pass, the anglers boarded the rowboats and the boats were cut free from the *Valima*. When a tarpon was hooked, the guide did his best to row for the Boca Grande Lighthouse on the north side of the pass, where the angler fought the fish from the shore. (Courtesy of the Gasparilla Inn.)

A "daisy chain" of 11 rowboats from Useppa are towed by the *Valima* to Boca Grande Pass for tarpon fishing, c. 1905. (Courtesy of the Gasparilla Inn.)

Guests of the Gasparilla Inn are pictured with their catch of the day and their fishing guide, c. 1920. Many women, in their prim Edwardian dresses, fought and caught tarpon. (Courtesy of the Gasparilla Inn.)

Florida railroad magnate Henry Plant was photographed with this large tarpon. (Courtesy of the Gasparilla Inn.)

With the mass production of gasoline engines after 1910, guides could now reach the pass on their own power in boats such as the one in this c. 1930 postcard. The early powerboats were open boats, but they were bigger and safer than rowboats. The numbers of anglers increased. In the background are the local tarpon guides' boathouse and quarters on Boca Grande Bayou. (Courtesy of the *Boca Beacon*.)

The buildings in this c. late 1950s postcard of the "Boat House and Guide Quarters, Boca Grande, Fla." no longer exist. (Courtesy of the *Boca Beacon*.)

This 1924 postcard shows Boca Grande entrepreneur and businessman Jerome Fugate with a 155-pound tarpon caught in Boca Grande Pass. (Courtesy of the *Boca Beacon*.)

An angler in an open boat fights a leaping "silver king" in Boca Grande Pass in front of the Boca Grande Lighthouse in this c. 1938 postcard. (Courtesy of the *Boca Beacon*.)

Fabled tarpon guide Capt. Phalo Padilla is pictured with a satisfied lady angler, c. 1950. (Courtesy of the Gasparilla Inn.)

This stylized c. 1940s postcard says, "Hooked, the tarpon leaps to the surface in Florida waters." (Courtesy of the *Boca Beacon*.)

Capt. Sam Whidden, the founder of the famous Whidden's Marina in Boca Grande, hauls in a big tarpon. The marina that Captain Whidden established in 1926 and that still bears his name continues to serve the boating public today. It is run by his daughters, Isabelle Whidden Joiner and Barbara Whidden Chatham. (Courtesy of the *Boca Beacon*.)

Sleek wooden cabin cruisers like this tarpon boat didn't become common until the 1950s. Capt. Rayford "Sug" Futch, seen here, is in the bayou on his way to the pass about 1950. The boat, the *Old Crow*, was built by John D. Riggs in Punta Gorda in the mid-1930s. (Courtesy of Capt. Mark Futch.)

Tarpon weren't the only big fish to provide a sporting thrill for early anglers. There were sharks, sawfish, giant jewfish, and even stingrays, one of which is shown here, having been harpooned for sport, c. 1902. (Courtesy of the Boca Grande Historical Society.)

Golf was, and remains, a favorite pastime in Boca Grande, which had two golf courses for a time—one at the Gasparilla Inn and one at the Boca Grande Hotel. (Courtesy of Pansy Polk Cost.)

Basketball was a popular school sport, and this is the 1934 team. Boca Grande School sports teams had to travel by boat or ferry to the mainland for away games. When teams played games as far away as Everglades City, they left in the afternoon and often would not get home until daybreak of the next day. (Courtesy of Jeff Gaines.)

Not to be outdone by the boys, Boca Grande School's girls had a basketball team. They are seen here practicing. (Courtesy of the *Boca Beacon*.)

Boca Grande School's football team, the Tarpons, won the Florida State Championship in 1938, 1939, and 1940. This is the 1940 team. (Courtesy of the *Boca Beacon*.)

EPILOGUE

The building of the Boca Grande Causeway signaled the end of an era and the beginning of another for Gasparilla Island. Passenger train service to the island ended shortly after the causeway was completed in 1958. By 1960, the fishing village of Gasparilla was a relic. The Boca Grande School closed in 1964. The last ship carrying phosphate from Port Boca Grande sailed in 1979. The African-American community was gone by the mid-1980s. The island's socio-economic balance was undergoing a transformation.

In 1980, the Florida legislature, with the support of local citizens (the Gasparilla Island Conservation and Improvement Association) and legislators, passed the Gasparilla Island Conservation District Act. The act significantly curtailed development by limiting the height of structures and density of dwellings per acre. It also froze the zoning in place at the time and limited on-site signage. CSX Resources, the development arm of CSX Inc. (successor to Seaboard Coast Line Railroad), began building its Boca Bay development at mid-island and at the south end in the late 1980s, and Sunset Realty Corp. began to develop the north end of the island. Along with development came restoration and preservation. The school became a community center. The railroad depot, the theater, the old powerhouse, and the lighthouse were all restored and now serve new purposes. The Sharp family, which had acquired the railroad right-of-way from CSX Corporation, donated it to the community for a bicycle path. The same family donated a mile of beachfront and 113 acres of property at the south end of the island to the state of Florida for a state park. And in 1989 all of downtown Boca Grande became a Lee County Historic District.

Despite many changes, people who choose to call Boca Grande home today cherish it for the same reasons that people have since the days when fishermen and then, railroad officials, first recognized its special magic, its natural beauty, wonderful climate, world-class fishing, and its isolation from, yet proximity to the "mainland world." Boca Grande's first residents treasured the island for its unspoiled beauty and later, for its wonderful diversity, and began a special way of life that continues to this day.

SELECTED BIBLIOGRAPHY

Abbott, Karl P. *Open for the Season*. Garden City, New York: Doubleday, 1950.

Arnold, Anthony Brown. *A Brief History of Boca Grande*. Unpublished manuscript, November 1951.

Boca Grande Historical Society. "How It All Began." Unpublished monograph by Theodore B. VanItallie, prepared in connection with the Society's 1997 exhibition of historic photographs.

Boca Grande Historical Society. *Connections*. Vol. 1, No. 1, 1999, and Vol. 1, No. 2, 1999.

Department of Commerce and the National Oceanographic and Atmospheric Administration, *Tropical Cyclones of the North Atlantic Ocean, 1871–1992*.

Edic, Robert F. *Fisherfolk of Charlotte Harbor, Florida*. Gainesville, FL: Institute of Archeology and Paleoenvironmental Studies, University of Florida, 1996.

Ffolliott, Peter. *Sea Wall History: First to Fourth Street in Boca Grande*. Unpublished manuscript, 1994.

Gibson, Charles Dana. *Boca Grande: A Series of Historical Essays*. Great Outdoors Publishing Co.: 1982.

Ingram, Michael. *A Title Examiner's History of Boca Grande*. Boca Grande, FL: The Boca Beacon, 1996.

Johnson, Carey. *Boca Grande, The Early Days: Memoirs of an Island Son*. Boca Grande, FL: Barrier Island Parks Society, 1990.

Turner, Gregg M. *Railroads of Southwest Florida*. Charleston, SC: Arcadia Publishing, 1999.

Williams, Lindsey, and U.S. Cleveland. *Our Fascinating Past. Charlotte Harbor: The Early Years*. Punta Gorda, FL: Charlotte Harbor Area Historical Society, 1993.

Williams, Lindsey, and U.S. Cleveland. *Our Fascinating Past. Charlotte Harbor: The Later Years*. Punta Gorda, FL: Charlotte Harbor Area Historical Society, 1996.

www.ingramcontent.com/pod-product-compliance
Lightning Source LLC
Chambersburg PA
CBHW080850100426
42812CB00007B/1979